Sad Man
Second in the series of th
John Gammon Peak District Crim

A Detective Mystery by C J Galtrey.

This book is a work of fiction. Names, characters, organisations, places, events and incidents are either products of the author's imagination or are used fictitiously.

C J Galtrey.

Sad Man
Second in the series of the
John Gammon Peak District Crime Thrillers

Bixton seemed to be the last place God had decided to build - it was always cold and the first place in England to get snow, whilst a pretty town, it felt miserable.

John Gammon, or Superintendent Gammon as he was now known, was sat at his desk pondering. It had been a year since his brother had chosen to take the law into his own hands and walk into a pub in Derby that was frequented by some pretty unsavoury characters and started shooting them. He killed all of the main players that had been involved in the case that had brought Gammon back to Derbyshire to help with the investigations.

John Gammon was now divorced from the blood-sucking Lindsay; he had a brief affair with Jeannette Goslyarnee an old friend; then he let work come into his private and work life. Both Gammon and Chief Constable, Vicky Wills, knew from the start that it would be a mistake, but they had a passion for each other, which ultimately cost Wills her position as Chief Constable.

They thought that their affair was kept well away from work but they had been seen out together more than once by Susan Alexander who lived in Derbyshire and was Head of the Police Complaints Committee. She didn't get on well with Wills so they were quite sure that it had got passed on higher up the food chain and Wills was transferred to Somerset - same job, Chief Constable - but they both knew why. Gammon was then passed over for her position and that was given to Max Allen.

Just as Superintendent Gammon stood up and looked out of his office window across at the beautiful Peaks and Dales, there was a knock on the door. 'Come in,' Gammon shouted.

'Sorry to bother you, Sir, but we have a reported rape downstairs that may interest you.'

'No problem, Sergeant Hanney, which interview rooms is she in?'

'Number two, Sir, with Inspector Scooper and Inspector Evans.'

'Ok, I will be there in a minute.'

Gammon thought this would have been something Scooper and Evans should be able to handle. Little did he know, the enormity this case was about to bring. As Gammon walked down the stairs he could see a big thick-set guy looking agitated. 'Can I help you, Sir?'

'I doubt it, that is unless you can speak with Claire and tell her this rape charge is a load of rubbish?'

'And why would I do that?'

Sad Man
Second in the series of the
John Gammon Peak District Crime Thrillers

'You know what these teenagers are like - I kept saying to her to use the extra money Claire gave her for a taxi.'

'Ok, Mr…?'

'Reynolds, Jim Reynolds.'

'Why don't you calm down, get yourself a cup of coffee while I speak with your daughter and see if we can get the bottom of what has happened?'

Gammon carried onto interview room two. Scooper stopped the tape and addressed the tape machine. 'Superintendent Gammon is entering the room. Time 3.38pm, April 2nd, 2015.' The poor girl sat across from Gammon looked dreadful; she had mud in her hair and blood on her nose. She looked like she had been pulled through a hedge backwards.

'What's your name? We are here to help you, Dana. I am Superintendent John Gammon, Dana. Ok, Dana, tell me exactly what happened.'

Dana's word struggled to come out of her trembling mouth. 'I left the Shuffle night club in Bixton at about 2.45am this morning, my friend Sarah had met a guy so I had nobody to go home with. I walked along Bridge Street and as I passed the old bakery on the corner where there is a small alleyway, from out of the alleyway...' at this point she started to cry.

'Would you like a drink, Dana?' In a broken voice she replied she would be ok.

'Just take your time.' Gammon then noticed all up her arms were scratches. 'Dana, do you self-harm?'

'No, definitely not, this man had a full length coat on with what I saw to be barbed wire attached so I could not fight him off. I screamed and he placed something over my mouth and the next thing I knew, I woke up in this ploughed field and the man was on top of me.'

'Did you see his face, Dana?' She started to cry again.

'Just take your time, we are here to help you.'

She composed herself again. 'He had a ski mask on, I could hear him laughing.'

'Ok, Dana, we are arranging for a nurse to get you cleaned up and get you examined, then you can speak with the abuse counsellor. Interview terminated 4.01pm.'

The nurse came and took Dana away, then Gammon spoke with both Evans and Scooper. 'I don't want the press hearing about this just yet, are you clear on that?'

'Yes, Sir.'

'See if we can speak with Mr Reynolds - I didn't like the way he seemed. Put him in interview room one. I will be there shortly.' Scooper and Evans asked Jim Reynolds to have a chat in interview room one. He seemed very agitated at this but did agree to it.

Gammon stepped outside and spoke with Dana's mother. 'She is in good hands, Mrs Reynolds.'

'My name is Bryant, Claire Bryant.'

'Oh, I am sorry, I thought Dana was Mr Reynolds' daughter.'

'No, we just live together - Dana's father left many years ago and I met Jim about three months ago.'

'Ok, Claire, is it ok if I call you Claire?'

'Yes, Mr Gammon.'

'We are going to speak to Mr Reynolds, and then I would like a chat with you. Would you like the desk sergeant to get you a cup of tea?'

'No, I will be fine, thank you for your kindness.'

Sad Man
Second in the series of the
John Gammon Peak District Crime Thrillers

Gammon made his way to interview room one. 'Are you ok to have a chat, Mr Reynolds, without a solicitor?'

'I haven't done anything - it's the way these bloody kids dress, they are inviting trouble.'

'I believe you are not Dana's father?'

'No.'

'I am also guessing you are not local from your accent.'

'I am from the North East, I met Claire when I was lorry-driving, she works in the truck stop - we hit it off so I moved down here.'

'Where do you work now?'

'I drive for Witters in Swinster.'

'Ok, and where were you this morning?'

'I had been drinking in Bixton and to be honest had a few too many so slept it off in the car before driving home.'

'What time did you arrive home?'

'It must have been around 10.30am this morning.'

'Can anybody vouch for you, Mr Reynolds?'

Sad Man
Second in the series of the
John Gammon Peak District Crime Thrillers

'I'm not sure, I was drinking in the Spread Eagle but it was busy and I don't really know anyone, having only been here a few months.'

'Did you know Dana was in Bixton?'

'No, we don't speak much. Don't think she likes me to be honest.'

'Ok, Mr Reynolds, we may need to question you again, so while the investigation is on-going you must report your whereabouts if you decide to leave the area.'

'What, even when I am driving my truck?'

'No, only if you leave the area you are living in now.'

'This is bloody silly, am I a suspect?'

'Everyone is a suspect, Mr Reynolds, until proven otherwise.' With that, Gammon left the interview room. It was a bad day to have all this on his doorstep - the replacement for Chief Constable Wills had started today and he had quite a reputation. Gammon decided he better go and fill Chief Constable Max Allen in on this case.

Gammon climbed the stairs to Chief Constable Allen's office. It wasn't more than nine months that he had been having a torrid affair with Chief

Sad Man
Second in the series of the
John Gammon Peak District Crime Thrillers

Constable Wills sometimes in that very office at night.

Gammon knocked on the door of Max Allen's office. 'Enter,' said the voice in the office. Max Allen stood up from behind his desk. Allen was a diminutive man and he had a scar, which ran from his left ear, across the bridge of his nose to the corner on the right hand side of his mouth. Gammon had been led to believe that Allen had tackled a Birmingham gangster when he had gone to arrest in a bookmakers on Lipton Street in Birmingham - a notorious place and not a place for the faint hearted, which Allen certainly was not. Allen did arrest the guy who was six feet two inches tall and he was only five foot eight, and for his trouble, Mickey Campbell had pulled a blade on him.

Allen was not to be taken lightly. He had taken the post at Bixton as Chief Constable after Wills had left.

'Sit down, so you are the famous John Gammon, hey laddie?'

'Hardly famous, Sir.'

'Oh, I think so, I have heard a lot about the shining star of the Derbyshire Constabulary and formerly of the Met. Let me tell you something, laddic.' Gammon could sense this wasn't going well. 'You are now under my command and my rules - I don't have mavericks on my team, I expect you to report every detail of every case you work, do not try and run alone or I will have you stopping motorist for speeding fines quicker than you can say Horace Wimpole, are we clear?' Unsure what the reference to Horace Wimpole was Gammon thought it best to agree.

'Completely, Sir.'

'Right, who are your officers?'

'Inspector Scooper - a very good officer, very committed to getting the job done; Inspector Evans - a local man with a lot of knowledge of the area; Sergeant Paul Bradbury; Sergeant Paul Bannon and Sergeant Carl Milton. Bradbury and Bannon had been at Bixton for only about three months when the other Detective Inspectors moved on and Carl Milton was in the Rapid Response team in Derby, which he was commended to twice.

'Yes, I know, Gammon, his girlfriend was killed and he acted alone bloody fool.'

'I think there was circumstances involved, Sir, he is a very good officer.'

'I will be the judge of that.'

'Anyone else?'

Sad Man
Second in the series of the
John Gammon Peak District Crime Thrillers

'Lee Hanney is the desk sergeant and we have PC Diane Trimble. That is the full complement, Sir.'

'Ok, so quite low on numbers then, Gammon.'

'I think so, Sir, but I guess I am biased.'

'Yes, I guess you are. I have requested a guy who worked with me before in Bristol - his name is Dave Smarty - he is an inspector and a bloody good officer other than he never shuts up about his beloved Manchester City so I am hoping to get him transferred up here.' Gammon knew straight away that Smarty would be the eyes and ears of Allen.

'Right, what cases are you working on?'

'We have a suspected rape case with a bizarre twist - apparently the girl who is claiming she was raped said the guy wore a ski mask and a coat with barbed wire sewn into it so she could not get a hold on him. The other case I am working on is in Derby - you are probably aware of the suspected serial killings a year ago and the involvement of my brother.'

'Yes, Gammon, what is it with people round here who take the law into their own hands? You can leave the briefing about that for now, I have a meeting with Sir John Staple, the High Sheriff of Derbyshire, at 2pm so I need to prepare for that. Shut the door on your way out.'

Sad Man
Second in the series of the
John Gammon Peak District Crime Thrillers

Gammon was seething inside, *what an obnoxious little Scottish twerp.*

The results were back from Dana's examination - she had been raped but there was no DNA, this guy knew exactly what he was doing.

Gammon decided it was best he broke the news to Dana's Mum, Claire Braint. 'Sergeant Hanney, can you get me a tea for Mrs Braint please. Claire, would you like to come into this room please.'

Gammon took Claire into his office and called Inspector Scooper to also attend. 'Shut the door please, Scooper.'

'Is it bad, Mr Gammon?'

'I am afraid Claire, your daughter, was raped by this person, we have just had the results through.' Claire broke down crying, Scooper put her arm round her. 'We can arrange for counselling for you and Dana if you wish, Claire.'

'I don't want counselling, I want this bastard caught.'

'I will do everything in my power to fulfil your wish, Claire, I can assure you of that. I may need to speak to you further in the next few days, Claire, would that be ok?'

'Yes, Mr Gammon, why was Jim spoken with?'

Sad Man
Second in the series of the
John Gammon Peak District Crime Thrillers

'It's just routine at the moment, Claire.'

'He was very angry about it and stormed off home.'

'Has he got a violent temper then, Claire?'

Claire paused for a moment, 'He did hit me once, he didn't mean and it he was very sorry afterwards, Mr Gammon.'

'Ok, Claire, you have enough on your plate at the moment. Scooper, can you take Claire and Dana home? I will be in touch, Claire.'

'Thank you for being so kind, Mr Gammon.'

Claire and Dana followed Scooper out of the station and left Gammon pondering over Jim Reynolds. It was now 6.00pm and Gammon felt he needed a quick drink to relax. After he and Jeannette had split up, Gammon had rented a cottage near his parents' farm so he could keep an eye on them after the trauma of his brother.

Gammon left work and drove to the Spinning Wheel in Swinster. As he walked into the bar he was met by Kev, the landlord, in his red dickie bow - cheery as always. 'How's Mr Gammon tonight?'

'Not bad, Kev, just been a long day, what have you got on to excite my palette?'

'Try this one, John, it's from Hittington-in-the-Dale microbrewery - they call it Belly Wobbler.'

Sad Man
Second in the series of the
John Gammon Peak District Crime Thrillers

'Go on then, why not.'

'Three pounds ten pence please, John.'

'That's a very good drink, Kev.'

'Have you seen much of your mate?'

'Who Lineman, Kev?'

'Yeah, that cheeky buggar.'

'Think he is all loved up, we haven't been out for a couple of months, think he is quite busy on Jo Wicket's place.'

'That will be some place hey, John, when it's finished.'

'You're not wrong there, Kev.'

'Now then, my lovely, how are you tonight? Are you eating?'

'Not tonight, Doreen, just having a quick pint and got to catch up on some paperwork at home.'

'Well, you make sure you eat, or I will be cross with you.'

'I will, Doreen, I promise.' Gammon sat at the end of the bar as the pub slowly filled up with early doors drinkers.

Sad Man
Second in the series of the
John Gammon Peak District Crime Thrillers

Tony Sherriff and his wife Rita, with Jackie and Cheryl came in. 'Hi John,' Cheryl shouted across. John put his hand up.

From out of the snug bar he heard the dulcet tones of Carol Lestar, 'Are you coming in here to sit with me, John?'

'Would love to, Carol, but I have a stack of paperwork to get through at home so I am finishing this, then I'm off.'

'Ok, you miserable buggar,' and she laughed.

Gammon finished his beer, said goodbye to everyone and left the pub. He climbed into his beloved Jaguar and set off for his cottage. Once home, he made a cup of coffee and sat down with his pile of paperwork - this part of the job he hated. After wading through the mountain of paperwork Gammon detested, it was now 12.38am and Gammon decided it was time he went to bed.

Climbing the stairs, the picture he had on the wall of his brother and himself haymaking when they were little boys brought back so sad memories. How had Adam and John become so distanced and then just when they were getting to know each other again Adam kills himself?

Gammons bedroom was immaculate as was the house - he was a very tidy person - everything had its place. This detail he took into his career as a police officer.

Gammon settled down and was soon in a deep sleep. He was woken at 4.30 am by his mobile ringing - it was Inspector Scooper. 'Sir, sorry to bother you, but there has been another possible rape, and speaking with the victim, it seems to be the same format.'

'I'm on my way. Meet me at the scene, Scooper, get Evans and Milton to take the victim to Bixton station. Where was the scene of the crime?'

'It's in Micklock, Sir, on the moor - if you drive on the moor you will see a big house, it's the only one for miles, I will meet you at the gate at the bottom of the drive.'

Gammon quickly dressed. He locked the front door and put the key under the stone by the water feature. Mrs Broadshaw cleaned today and Gammon often forgot to leave the key so they decide this was the best place.

Gammon drove with some haste to Micklock moor following Scooper's instruction and after about a mile he could see Scooper's car at the gates of an old run down mansion.

Sad Man
Second in the series of the
John Gammon Peak District Crime Thrillers

When Gammon pulled up, the sun was coming up behind the mansion, which made it all the more creepy. 'What have we got, Scooper?'

'It appears our man has struck again. The lady that lived here is in her eighties, she is the daughter of a local Hydro magnet Sir Michael Alison - he owned three Hydros in Micklock in the boom days and Meredith Alison is the only surviving child. She said she was woken by the sound of somebody crying and there was loud banging coming from the downstairs kitchen porch. She said she put her dressing gown on and went downstairs and to her horror there was a young girl of about twenty years of age all dishevelled, standing covered in mud, crying for help.'

'Ok, let's go and see Miss Alison.'

'Be surprised, Sir, the house is like something out of Dickens's Great Expectations.' They knocked on the front door and an impatient voice shouted to come round the back so Gammon and Scooper duly followed the instruction. Gammon's first sight of Miss Alison took him back, she stood there in a long Victorian-like dress, she had small round glasses on and what looked like lace gloves with no fingers in them.

'Superintendent Gammon, Bixton Police, Miss Alison. I believe you have met Inspector Scooper.'

Sad Man
Second in the series of the
John Gammon Peak District Crime Thrillers

'Come in, come in,' she said, 'It's cold with the door open.'

'Would you mind answering a few questions?'

'What, more questions? I have just told this young lady not half an hour ago everything I know.'

'Let's just try, just in case you have forgotten anything, Miss Alison.'

'What time did you hear the commotion?'

'I don't know, I don't have clocks - they are a waste of time. What would I need a clock for? I'm just waiting to meet my maker and I don't need a clock for that.' Gammon could feel this wasn't going well.

'How would you describe the young lady that you met at your door?'

'I would say she was about twenty-two but it's hard to tell, they all dress like strumpets.'

Scooper gave a flash of a smile to Gammon. 'Was she dishevelled in any way?'

'Her skirt and blouse was torn, mind there wasn't much skirt to tear, I thought anyway. She had mud in her hair and she was covered in cuts on her arms and legs.'

'What did she say to you, Miss Alison?'

Sad Man
Second in the series of the
John Gammon Peak District Crime Thrillers

'She said she had been attacked and could I help her. It was a dam good job she had one of those hand phones to call you lot because I don't have a phone.'

'She put the number in and I spoke to somebody at Bixton police station.'

'Is there anything else you can add?'

'No, nothing, oh, just one thing, she said he wore a ski mask with red lips, she could have been delirious for all I know.'

'Ok, thank you for your time, Miss Alison,' and with that, Gammon and Scooper left the house.

'Blimey, she was a strange woman, Sandra.'

'Certainly was, Sir.'

'Right, let's get back to Bixton, have you organised for a doctor to see the girl?'

'Yes, Sir, should have results by the time we get back to the station.'

'Were you at the station when the call came through?'

'Yes, Sir.'

'How come you were at work so early?'

'I was just catching up on paperwork, Sir.'

Sad Man
Second in the series of the
John Gammon Peak District Crime Thrillers

'Ok, but remember I need my officers fresh, and trying to do too many hours will not help you be fresh and alert. Taken it on board?'

'Ok, Sir, thanks.'

Gammon and Scooper arrived at Bixton station. Hanney, the desk Sergeant, said that the doctor was waiting in Gammon's office. 'Ok, thanks Sergeant.'

'Scooper, you take the victim into interview room one, get her a coffee and I will be with you shortly.'

Doctor Mycock was a local guy and had been John Gammon's family doctor so Gammon knew him well. 'Good morning, doctor.'

'Yes, good morning, John, I have the report on Miss Peterson - I am afraid she has been sexually assaulted, there is a lot of bruising so it appears that it wasn't consensual. She is in a very bad state, John.'

'Ok, Doctor Mycock, thanks for that, was there anything we can get DNA from?'

'No, he appears very clever, John.'

'Thanks, Doctor.'

'Give my regards to your parents when you see them, John.'

Sad Man
Second in the series of the
John Gammon Peak District Crime Thrillers

'I will, Doctor.' Gammon left his office and went straight down to interview room one.

On entering the interview room Scooper addressed the tape machine, 'Superintendent John Gammon has now entered the interview room, time is 6.41pm, Wednesday 2nd April, 2014.'

Scooper passed Gammon her notes. 'Milan, that's a pretty name, Miss Peterson, do you mind if I call you Milan?'

'Milan Peterson was silent for a second as she held back her tears, 'Yes, that's ok, Sir.'

'Tell you what, you call me John, then, and I will call you Milan.' Milan nodded in agreement.

The doctor had cleaned Milan up but her arms and legs were badly cut and the poor girl looked dreadful. 'Would you like us to call your parents?'

After what seemed like an age, Milan spoke. 'My Mum and Dad are in Tenerife on holiday until today, they are retired, they had me when they were quite old.'

'Is there anyone else you would like us to contact?'

'No, I don't want anyone to know about this.'

'Ok, Milan, but I do need to ask you some awkward questions. Did you know your attacker?'

Sad Man
Second in the series of the
John Gammon Peak District Crime Thrillers

'No, he had a ski mask with red lips and he kept laughing while he was hurting me,' at this Milan broke down crying uncontrollably.

'Gather yourself, Milan, have a drink of your coffee, if we are to get this monster I have to have as much detail that you can give me.'

'I understand, John.'

'Ok, Milan, let's try again - run through your night for me.'

'It was my friend's birthday, so we had been for a meal at the Wobbly Man in Toad Holes then Judy, my friend, said let's get a taxi to Bixton and spend the night there. I wasn't bothered but could not say no with it being Judy's birthday.'

'What was the name of the taxi company you used?'

'I remember it because it was called Joe Le Taxis, which I remember thinking was quite funny.'

'How many went to Bixton? Can you give us the names as well, Milan?'

'There was me, Judy Skills, Carrie Boytock, Mia Thorne, Angela Russock, Trish Thurlow and Suzy Warner so seven of us and the taxi company sent a mini bus.'

'How did you find the driver?'

Sad Man
Second in the series of the
John Gammon Peak District Crime Thrillers

'He was a bit creepy - he was making comments about our skirts.'

'What sort of comments?'

'Well, he said to Angela that he had a handkerchief bigger then her skirt and he told Trish she had great legs.'

'Did say anything to you?'

'He said something like I was a ripe apple - don't know what he meant by that.'

'What did the taxi driver look like?'

'He was foreign and he had dark skin, not bad looking - a bit like these bar men you see on holiday in Spain.'

'Did he have a name?'

'I remember now, he gave Suzy Warner his mobile number and he wrote his name on the card - I think he said it was something like Ludo.'

'Ok, thanks for that, Milan.'

'You don't think he had anything to do with this, do you?'

'I don't know, Milan, everyone is a suspect until we have it sorted. Right explain to me how this came about.'

Sad Man
Second in the series of the
John Gammon Peak District Crime Thrillers

'Well, we had a drink in the Spread Eagle, most young people congregate there - they have cheap drinks all night.'

'Did you speak with anyone in there?'

'Yes, quite a few there - was Dave Neilson, I was at school with Dave.'

'Where does he live?'

'He lives in Swinster with his Mum and Dad, number three Cherry Crescent, I think. Then I spoke with another couple of guys but by now I was feeling a bit drunk. Oh yes, an older guy, I think he said his name was Jimmy, he was a Geordie and he asked me to dance but I said no. He grabbed my arm and said did I want to go outside, luckily Suzy was coming back from the toilets so she asked if I was ok and the creep let go and disappeared into the crowd - I never saw him again.

'We left the Spread Eagle about 1.30pm. Suzy and Trish had copped off so it left me, Judy and Carrie so we went for a Kebab.'

'Did you speak with anyone in the Kebab house?'

'No, not really but I did see that creep again - he had his arms everywhere round this woman, they were walking out of the Kebab shop as we walked in and he did stare at us'.

Sad Man
Second in the series of the
John Gammon Peak District Crime Thrillers

'So what happened next?'

'Judy phoned her Dad and he dropped Mia off at Swinster then he took me home to Micklock. I live down a big drive so he dropped me off at the top. I thanked him and he drove off. I was walking down the drive and it's quite poorly lit,' at this point Milan broke down again.

'Take a minute, Milan.' Scooper put her arm around Milan's shoulders. Milan composed herself and started to tell the story.

'I felt something go over my mouth and heard that laugh, I felt very drowsy then the next thing I remember is being in a muddy field and I was coming round and could feel something heavy on me and it was this maniac. I tried to fight him off but he just laughed at me, he had something sharp all round his coat and I could not get hold of him, he was just laughing.'

'Did he speak at all?'

'No, he just laughed. He then hit me and I was knocked out. I woke in the field and he was gone so I stood up but still felt in a daze and I could see the big house where Miss Alison lives. I knew it because as kids we would go scrumping there for apples. I ran and ran until I got to her door, she came to the door and I gave her my phone to phone the police.'

Sad Man
Second in the series of the
John Gammon Peak District Crime Thrillers

'Ok, Milan, well done, would you like my officer to stay with you tonight at your house?'

'My parents are back this morning - in fact they are probably back now, they were landing at East Midlands at 7.45am.'

'Ok, Milan, Inspector Scooper will take you home and explain the situation to your parents and we will be in touch.'

'Thank you, Mr Gammon, for being so kind.'

'No problem, Milan, thank you for being so brave, we will catch this animal, trust me.' Gammon left the interview room as Scooper stopped the tape.

Climbing the stairs to his office, he met Max Allen coming out of his office, 'Another bloody problem, Gammon?'

'You could say that, Sir.'

'Well, I have good news, Dave Smarty will be joining us tomorrow from Bristol - he is an excellent officer, Gammon, everything by the book, that's Smarty.'

'Oh that's good then, Sir.'

'Yes, I said you would pick him up from Bixton train station at 9am - he will get things moving you can be sure of that.' *Great,* thought Gammon *all I need - a bloody mole in the camp.*

Sad Man
Second in the series of the
John Gammon Peak District Crime Thrillers

Gammon sat in his office thinking over what Milan had said especially about the Geordie guy called Jimmy and the taxi driver, Ludo something, wasn't ringing true.

'Sergeant Milton, you're coming with me.'

'Ok, Sir where are we going?'

'Witter transport in Swinster. Wipe your shoes before you get in my Jag, I don't want mud on the cream carpets.'

'Yes, Sir.'

Gammon decided this was a good time to get to know Carl - he seemed like a shy officer. 'Now then, Sergeant, how about you tell me a bit about yourself?'

'Not a lot to tell, Sir. I live in Toad Holes, I have a small cottage and a springer spaniel, I enjoy walking and that's about it.'

'You were previously in Rapid Response in Derby - why did you give that up?'

'With all due respect, Sir, you already know all this.'

'Yes, I do, Sergeant, but what I want to know is - do you still have the bottle for the job?'

'Yes, I do, Sir, it was just that internal thought it best if I was taken out of firearms because of the trauma caused and because I lost my girlfriend in the incident.'

'Trust me, Carl, I only want to be sure you can handle a pressured situation, so can you?'

'Yes I can, Sir, I am a professional police officer and want to serve. You will have no problems with me, Sir.'

'Good, glad to hear it, Carl, I like to know I have a team that looks out for each other.'

'To be honest, Sir, I could have stayed as a Sergeant in Derby but you are well known and I wanted to learn off you.'

'Ok, so here starteth the first lessons, Carl.'

Swinster was about fifteen miles from Bixton but by the time they reached Witters haulage yard, Gammon had pretty much worked out his thoughts on Sergeant Carl Milton.

They pulled into the yard. In front was a big garage with what looked like two big lorries with the mechanics with their heads in the engines. A small, red sign showed the way to reception. They entered the reception and rung the bell as instructed. A glass, sliding window was pushed across and a young lady in her early thirties smiled and asked if she could help. Gammon and Milton showed their warrant cards and asked to see

Andrew Witter or Clive Witter, one of the owners. 'I am afraid Mr Andrew and Mr Clive are away on business but Matt Gregory, the transport manager, is here.'

'Ok, we will see Mr Gregory.'

'What is it concerning?'

'If you just tell him we are following up on some information we require on a current case please.'

The receptionist showed Gammon and Milton into the Transport manager's office. Gregory was a heavy smoker and the air was thick with cigarette smoke. He was a big guy, possibly six foot two and about eighteen stone but not particularly overweight.

'How can I help you, chaps?' They sat down and started to ask questions about Jim Reynolds. The first thing Gammon noticed was Gregory calling Reynolds 'Jimmy'.

'Do you know Mr Reynolds as Jim or Jimmy, Mr Gregory?'

'I have always known him as Jimmy, why, what is this about?'

'It isn't something I can elaborate on at this time, we just need to check a few things. Does Mr Reynolds have any friends here at Witters Transport, you know, like guys he goes drinking with?'

'Not really, Jimmy is a good worker, will always do the overtime but he doesn't mix particularly well.'

'Have you ever had any trouble with Mr Reynolds?'

'Just once when he first started, one of the guys, Mark Rhodes, said something like 'all Geordies are dicks' or something as he had been to buy a car from Sunderland that weekend and it was a wasted journey. It was just a throwaway line but Jimmy got all upset and took a swing at Mark knocking him into the side of the canteen. Luckily there was one or two in there and they stopped it before it got too ugly. Mark and Jimmy don't speak anymore but that's fine, they generally are on different routes anyway.

'Is Jimmy in trouble? Only he hasn't shown up for work these last two days.'

'Have you tried to contact him?'

'We rung his mobile - it rang but no answer and the house phone seems like it's been cut off.'

'Ok, Mr Gregory, thank you for your time, I'm sure it will be something and nothing with Jimmy. Thanks for your time.'

Sad Man
Second in the series of the
John Gammon Peak District Crime Thrillers

When Gammon and Milton got back in the car immediately Gammon said, 'Did you notice Gregory called Reynolds 'Jimmy'? That is what the last victim said the guy was called in the nightclub that pulled her arm.'

'Yes, Sir, I wrote it in my book.'

'Well done, Carl, we will make a detective of you yet. Righ,t we are off to speak with the taxi company, Joe Le Taxis.'

Gammon and Milton arrived at the taxi company - they could see the mini bus outside and also a couple of taxis. All the vehicles were white with 'Joe Le Taxi' emblazoned on the side.

They entered the small room where their drivers were sat and a woman was on the switchboard. 'Can I help you?' she said in a surly voice. 'If it's a taxi you want, they are all out and these people are before you so no chance for at least a half an hour.'

Gammon showed his warrant card and her mood changed - she seemed concerned. 'Look, we run legal here, I can show you all the paperwork.'

'Can we speak with the owner?'

'He is in Greece, he leaves me to run the taxis and only comes over every three months.'

Sad Man
Second in the series of the
John Gammon Peak District Crime Thrillers

'Ok, I need to speak with one of your taxi drivers, a guy called Ludo.'

'We don't have anybody called Ludo that works here.'

'Ok, who drove the mini bust from the Wobbly Man pub to Bixton last night?'

'Just a minute,' she drew heavily on her cigarette. 'Got it, that would have been Cristos, he is Mr Minolis's son.'

'When will he be back?'

'I am expecting him any minute.'

'What is the number plate of the vehicle he is driving?'

She scribbled the number down on a post-it note and handed it to Gammon. 'Ok, we will wait outside for him.'

'Do you want me to let him know?'

'No, just let him get here please.'

'Ok, officers.' Gammon and Milton stood outside and after about five minutes a taxi pulled into the yard.

'Mr Minolis?'

'Who is asking?'

Sad Man
Second in the series of the
John Gammon Peak District Crime Thrillers

'I'm Superintendent Gammon and this Sergeant Milton. We wonder if we could have a word with you.' At this, Minolis started to run away, Milton gave chase and brought him down with a superb rugby tackle. 'Well done, Carl, cuff him, we are taking him to the station.'

Cristos Minolis never spoke a word in the car. They arrived back at Bixton and put him in interview room two. Gammon started the tape, 'It's 3pm,' and proceeded to say the usual words to start the interview.

'Now, Cristos, why did you run away from us today?'

'No comment,' came the reply.

'Did you take a party of girls from the Wobbly Man in Toad Holes to the Spread Eagle in Bixton last night?'

'No comment.'

'Did you give a lady in the party a card with your mobile phone number and the name Ludo on it?'

'No comment.'

'This is not helping anybody, Cristos, we are investigating a serious allegation and you could have been a party to this or could have seen something that would help us find the culprit. Shall we start again - where do you live?'

'No comment.'

'Would you like a lawyer?'

'No Comment.'

'Ok. Cristos, I am arresting you for obstruction a police investigation - you don't have to say anything but if you don't this may harm your defence if this goes to court. Lock him up, Sergeant,' and with that Gammon switched off the tape. 'Come and see me, Milton, once the paperwork is cleared. I will be in my office.' Gammon climbed the stairs to his office. Max Allen was out so he sat pondering, *had they got the guy?* It just seemed too easy and the victims had no DNA on them from the culprit so this guy was smart and why was Minolis not willing to defend himself?

There was a knock on Gammon's door, 'Come in.'

'He is in one of the cells, Sir, how long can we keep him?'

'Forty eight hours, best leave him sweating tonight. You and Evans go round to the taxi company and get all his details where he lives, etc by 10.00am. We have a new Inspector who I am picking up from Bixton train station at 9.00am so I should be back to sort it by 10am.'

Sad Man
Second in the series of the
John Gammon Peak District Crime Thrillers

'Ok, Sir, leave that with me.'

'Good work today, Carl, cracking rugby tackle - have you played a bit?'

'I played for the police and represented England at under nineteen level some years ago, Sir.'

'Thought you must have played a bit.' Right, I'm calling it a day.'

'Goodnight, Sir.'

'Goodnight, Sergeant.' John drove back to his cottage in Hittington-in-the-Dale, he thought about going to see his parents but he thought he would get showered and go the Tow'd Man - he hadn't been in for a while with work commitments and since his brother died his Dad had not been the same, so he felt a little uncomfortable at his parents' house.

He showered and dressed arriving at the Tow'd Man for 8.00pm. 'Good evening. John.'

'Good evening, Denis, how are you and Clara?'

'Oh, she's normal, moaning at me but that's nothing new,' and he laughed. 'Where have you been? We've not seen you for all of two months.'

'Just a lot on at work.'

'Sad do about them girls getting raped, John, hey.'

Sad Man
Second in the series of the
John Gammon Peak District Crime Thrillers

'Sorry, Denis, what was that?'

'Have you not read the Micklock Mercury today? I'll get you one.' Gammon froze, *how the hell had the local rag got hold of this?* There on the front page was a picture of Dana leaving Bixton police station.

Gammon was furious but there was very little he could do now. 'Porky,' was the shout from main door entrance.

'Hiya Steve, hello Jo, how are you both?'

'We are good, John, what about you?'

'Well I was until I saw the Micklock Mercury.'

'Oh yeah, I saw that, John, how dreadful.'

'Yeah, it's not good, Jo, these girls are under enough pressure without the whole of the Dales knowing.

'Hey, Jo, leave John alone, he is out for the night.'

'She is ok, Steve, it's just annoying that's all.'

'Are we going to sit down? Lairy Bob and Cheryl are over there with Carol Lestar.'

Sad Man
Second in the series of the
John Gammon Peak District Crime Thrillers

'Ok, I'll follow you.'

'John, you come and sit with me and I can fill you in with all the gossip.'

'Oh, I can't wait Carol!'

The pub was slowly filling up. 'Is there a group on tonight, Bob?'

'Yeah, Steve, they call themselves Danni and Deidre and a Bowl Of Soup.'

'Wow, that sounds interesting.'

'Yeah I saw them at the Wobbly Man at Christmas - they were very good - they are a bit like the Pretenders, I guess.'

'How's the mansion coming on, Jo?'

'Flippin' hard work, Cheryl. Steve is doing a good job but the house has had so few repairs over the last twenty years that there is so much to do. Akins Builders have put a new roof on and you will never guess what they found in the loft - a trunk and in it was a letter from John Lennon to one of the previous owners thanking them for his stay! I am going to have it framed. There was also quite a lot of Beatles memorabilia, don't know what that would be worth '

'Exciting times hey, Jo?'

Sad Man
Second in the series of the
John Gammon Peak District Crime Thrillers

'Very much so, Cheryl, how's the shop going?'

'Really busy - Jackie has been poorly for about two weeks so Bob's Mum has been helping me - best move we made - going to Dilley Dale Ices we have tripled our turnover.'

The music started with a rendition of Chain Gang by the Pretenders and as usual, Denis indicated to anyone who came to the bar that they were too loud.

The night was soon over and Denis was calling time. Cheryl was very tipsy telling Bob what a cutie pie he was and poor Bob sat there in total oblivion trying to ignore Cheryl's advances. 'Ok well, I will see you all.'

'Hey, John, before you go, me and Jo have decided to get engaged and we wondered if you would all like to come to Up The Steps Maggie's - there will be about twenty of us if you all come. It's a fortnight on Saturday at 8pm, we are having a disco and a buffet.'

'Great,' they all said. Cheryl asked if it was ok if cutie pie came with her as she slipped down from her seat with Bob just rescuing her from the floor.

'Great, thanks everyone, we will see you there at 8pm then.' John left the pub and unwisely drove back to the cottage - he knew he was wrong but hey, life wasn't exactly a bowl of cherries at the moment.

He entered his cottage feeling quite lonely. John's life was not in a good place at the minute and he knew he had to get out of this rut. He poured himself a black coffee and sat at his small farmhouse table. Had he done right accepting the promotion and the job in Bixton? Had he done it more for his parents than for himself? He was over the Lindsay thing but he wasn't over his brother. The feeling that you let somebody down is not a feeling anybody wants to have the burden of but that is how John felt. It didn't matter how many times he heard 'you did your best for your brother' or 'you were not to blame', he knew deep down that he had let him down and he would have to live with that.

John finished his coffee, cleaned his teeth and climbed into bed. He wasn't long before he was in a deep sleep. John's alarm woke him just as the milkman was putting his milk on the step. It was now time for work and the wrath of Chief Constable Allen - he knew he would be the person to blame for the leak to the local rag on the rapes.

The drive to Bixton was always pleasant no matter what time of year it was with the beautiful sunrise and the shimmering shadows dancing on the Peaks and Dales, you could see why so many companies filmed round these parts.

He walked into Bixton station and Sergeant Hanney greeted him with his usual cheery morning greeting. 'Good morning, Sergeant.'

'Be careful, Sir, the Scotsman is on the rampage.' Hanney had no sooner got the words out of his mouth, when Allen's voice boomed from upstairs.

'Superintendent, my office, immediately.'

Gammon climbed the stairs and went into Allen's office. 'Now laddie, what the hell is going on?' and he threw the Micklock paper on the desk.

'What do you want me to say, Sir?'

'You could start by telling me who the bloody hell gave them the story.'

'I have no idea.' Gammon was starting to feel aggravated by Allen's posturing. 'Do you really think you can keep something like this out of the press? With due respect, Sir, these are small villages and they probably know more about the case than we currently do.'

'If that's the best you can come up with, Gammon, go and fetch Dave Smarty from the train station.'

Gammon just looked at him and left the office fuming has he went down the stairs. All the way over to fetch Smarty, John felt contempt for Allen and the man he was about to pick up from the station. Gammon arrived at the train station just as the train from Bristol carrying Dave Smarty arrived at platform three.

Gammon knew who he was straight away. Inspector Smarty was a tall guy, about fifty-seven with greying hair, quite long for a police officer. He had a Crombie-type coat with black trousers and shoes, a white shirt and a blue tie, but the thing that gave his identity away was the Manchester City football club scarf he had round his neck. Gammon approached him, 'Inspector Smarty?'

'Yes, are you Superintendent Gammon.'

'I am. Pleased to meet you, Sir.' Gammon couldn't bring himself to return the gesture as he was still fuming.

They walked to Gammon's car. As they set off, Smarty said something a little odd to Gammon. 'I haven't come up here as a mole for Max Allen Superintendent.'

'I sincerely hope not, Inspector, I have a good team and whoever comes in the team needs to fit in.'

'I will have no problem with that, Sir, that is of course on the assumption you don't have any officers that support Manchester United,' and he laughed.

'Think you are safe on that, think there is only Desk Sergeant Hanney and he is a big Derby County Fan.'

'Well somebody has to be, Sir,' and Smarty laughed again.

They landed at Bixton Police Station, Gammon got Smarty a coffee and called a meeting with all his officers. 'Ladies and gentlemen, this is Inspector Dave Smarty, he has transferred from Bristol to be here at Bixton. If you would all like to introduce yourselves.'

'Inspector Sandra Scooper.'

'Inspector Paul Evans.'

'Sergeant Carl Milton.'

'Police Constable Di Trimble.'

'The others are out, Sir.'

'Ok, Constable, thanks. Right, Dave, the main case we are throwing resources at is the rape of two local girls. Sergeant Milton, you take it from here - get Inspector Smarty up to speed. Scooper, you come with me - we are going to go and see Jim Reynolds again.'

Sad Man
Second in the series of the
John Gammon Peak District Crime Thrillers

They arrived at his house - it was on the large council estate at Micklock. The house looked like it was in need of some care and attention, the garden was unkempt - the fence dividing the semi-detached houses was broken and had never seen a paintbrush. Next door there was an ice cream van parked on the lawn and a gearbox out of a car. 'How do people live like this, Scooper?'

'Honestly don't know, Sir.'

They knocked on the door of 38 Paton's Road, Claire answered the door but only partially. 'Is Mr Reynolds in, Claire?'

'No, sorry, he has gone out.'

'Would it be ok if we came in for a few minutes?'

'Well, I am just about to go shopping.'

'It won't take a minute, Claire,' and they pushed their way in. As they got in the hallway, Gammon was quite surprised - it was very clean inside and nothing like its outside persona. As he looked up to speak to Claire, Sandra Scooper nudged him. 'What happened to your face, Claire?' All down the left side it was very badly bruised; her lip was cut and she had a black eye.

'I fell down the stairs the other day. Would you like a drink?'

Sad Man
Second in the series of the
John Gammon Peak District Crime Thrillers

'Tea would be nice please, Claire, white, no sugar.'

'Just a glass of water for me, please.'

'No problem, Inspector Scooper.'

Gammon and Scooper sat in the living room, which was tastefully decorated with lots of pictures of Dana, her brother and what looked like their father or maybe their grandfather. Claire arrived with the tea, water and a plate with some fig biscuits and rich tea biscuits all neatly displayed on a china plate.

'When will Mr Reynolds be back, Claire?'

At this Claire started crying and shaking, 'I don't know.'

'He did this to you, didn't he, Claire?'

She cried again but nodded her head to say yes. 'It happened after the interview you gave to him - he came home and was in a real nasty mean mood. He started on Dana saying that she dressed incorrectly and anything that had happened she had brought on herself so I just said 'Jim, leave her alone - can't you see how shaken she is?' and at that he went mad. He hit me several times round the head then he got the fire poker and hit me in the face with it, then he threw it down and stormed out. I haven't seen him since and that was three days ago.'

Sad Man
Second in the series of the
John Gammon Peak District Crime Thrillers

'He hasn't been at work either, Claire, we checked. Ok, well, if he does show, that's my card - call me.'

'I will, Mr Gammon.'

'How is Dana?'

'Oh, she has her good days, are you any closer to catching this man? I see it was in the Micklock newspaper.'

'We have several lines of inquiry - I will let you know when we make an arrest.' All the time John was talking he was thinking that her partner could be involved but he didn't want to pile anymore heartache on the poor woman.

'What now, Sir?'

'Back to the station, Scooper, let's see what the taxi driver has to say for himself now he has had twenty-four hours. Phone Sergeant Hanney - the taxi guy can get his lawyer in now so we aren't wasting time waiting for his legal representation.'

'Ok, Sir.'

They arrived back at the station to find that Hanney had put Cristos Minolis in interview room one. 'Send Dave Smarty down please, Sergeant Hanncy, I would like him to interview Cristos Minolis with me.' Smarty arrived just as Gammon was

Sad Man
Second in the series of the
John Gammon Peak District Crime Thrillers

putting on the tape. 'Its 4.10pm,' and he carried on with the usual spiel for the tape.

'Ok, Cristos, have you had time to think about the situation you are in?'

'I didn't do anything did I, Mr Wright?' Tony Wright was well known to Gammon - he was a local guy who took all the scumbag cases. He was about six feet four, well dressed he had done well for himself. He had a farm and ran a small donkey sanctuary in his spare time. *Quite apt,* Gammon thought.

'Look, Cristos, it is in your interest to cooperate with us.'

Wright nodded to Cristos, 'Ok, I'll tell you what happened, I did take the girls in the mini bus to the Spread Eagle in Bixton and I did give one of the girls my card with the name Ludo on it and my mobile number.'

'Why would you do that, Cristos? Why would you not use your correct name if you wanted to see the girl?'

'The problem is I am married and my father loves my three children - if my wife found out I see other girls she would divorce me and my father would make me go back home and quite likely take me out of his will.'

46

Sad Man
Second in the series of the
John Gammon Peak District Crime Thrillers

'So you have wasted police time because you are selfish and want to save your own skin. Do you know, for all we know, the real killer could have already raped another victim because of you. Get him out of my sight, be warned I am watching you,' and with that Gammon left the interview room.

Gammon went to his office, took his Paul Smith leather coat off the hook and decided to call it a night. Just as he was leaving Max Allen called him into his office. 'Update, laddie.' Gammon didn't need this tonight so he gave as good as he got.

'First things first, Chief Constable, I have a name - it's John, or Superintendent Gammon, not laddie. Secondly, I have only just left the interview room and your office was in darkness so I would have updated you in the morning.

'Little touchy, Gammon, how's Dave doing? He will be a major asset to this station he will climb the ranks pretty dam quick his potential is there for all to see.'

Gammon didn't react to the verbal rambling of the stupid man. 'Jim, or Jimmy Reynolds the boyfriend of the fist victim's mother seems to have disappeared - he hasn't been seen for three days. Sergeant Hanney has contactod all the police forces with a picture we had of him when he entered the station so hopefully we can be back in contact.'

Sad Man
Second in the series of the
John Gammon Peak District Crime Thrillers

'So you feel this Reynolds could be involved?'

'He is all I have at the moment, Sir, the other lead - a taxi driver, looks like he was just covering himself because he is married.'

'Well I need results, Gammon, and the clock is ticking.'

'Understand, Sir.' All the time he was talking to Allen, Dave Smarty was stood outside. Gammon opened the door to leave.

Allen invited Smarty in to the office, 'Com -e in, Dave, great to see you I was just telling Gammon what a great officer you are - he will have to watch his job.' Gammon threw a disconcerting glance at them both, said goodnight and left.

Driving home from Bixton Gammon could see the fields of small lambs with their mothers enjoying the evening sunshine. His mind changed to the pub and he decided he would have dinner at the Spinning Jenny in Swinster.

Gammon parked the Jaguar round the back - this was a habit he had started to do so nobody saw his car on the car park. He walked into the low beamed bar where Doreen met him, swiftly followed by a hug and a peck on the cheek. 'Oh hi, Doreen.' Gammon was taken aback by Doreen's over-the-top emotions.

Sad Man
Second in the series of the
John Gammon Peak District Crime Thrillers

'Are you and your Mum and Dad ok?'

'Well I can speak for me but not spoken to Mum and Dad for a couple of days, why?'

'Brian Lund is alive, John, wasn't he one of the men Adam shot in that pub in Derby?'

'But that's not possible, Doreen, I checked and I saw his face.'

'What you saw was Brian Lund's brother - Jerry Lund, they were twins apparently.'

'How do you know all this?'

'It's just been on Sky News - apparently Brian Lund is suing Derbyshire Police for not protecting him and his family.'

Kev poured John a double Brandy. 'Get that down you, lad, you look like you need it.' How was he going to tell his Mum and Dad had Adam died in vain? 'John, it's on the news again, look that's Brian Lund.' Lund was being interviewed outside the Drovers Arms where the shooting took place. Lund, dressed in a white tee shirt that could not hide his waistline and had written across the front 'Dam fine mess you made of that, Piggy'. The reference was Adam, John's brother, and piggy being the police.

Sad Man
Second in the series of the
John Gammon Peak District Crime Thrillers

This man has no shame, John thought. The interviewer asked why he had only just come out and said he was alive. Lund answered very calmly. 'The time wasn't right, Bixton police tried to pin all those murders on me and it was all because Inspector Gammon's brother used prostitutes and I knew some of the girls - they came in the Drovers quite often. I never hurt anyone, in fact I would often by them a drink when they came in, you have to feel sorry for these girls.' Gammon could not believe what he was hearing. Lund was flanked by three very big guys, all with their heads shaven to look menacing.

John kept thinking what this would do to his mother and father. 'I don't think I will have another drink, Doreen, thank you. I best go and see Mum and Dad.'

'No problem, John, hope you go on ok.'

John left the Spinning Jenny and drove over to the farm. As he was coming down the drive he could see blue flashing light and when he got closer he could see that it was an ambulance.

John pulled up sharply, jumped out of the car and ran over to see his mother being comforted by a paramedic. 'Mum, what's happened?'

'I found your Dad in the milking parlour - he was late for his tea and Roger Glazeback couldn't work tonight because he was going to some darts and dominoes presentation night. I went into the parlour - I had seen the news on Sky about that horrible man that your brother shot or we thought he had. Your Dad had the radio on and I am guessing he had heard this and they think he has had a heart attack.'

'Lock the house up Mum and we can follow the ambulance to the hospital.' John soon caught up with the ambulance and they followed the paramedics in. His Dad looked very pale and pretty motionless. A surly nurse told John and his mother to wait in the waiting room while his Dad was evaluated.

Almost two hours had passed when a doctor came out and asked John and his mother to go into a side office. 'Please sit, down my name is Mr Kinston, I attended your husband tonight, Mrs Gammon, I am afraid we did everything we could for him but he passed away. There was no more we could do, he had a massive heart attack and the chances for him surviving were very slim.' John's mother collapsed into John's arms. 'Take as much time as you need.'

'Thank you, Mr Kinston. John, what is happening to our family? First your brother, now your Dad. Your

Sad Man
Second in the series of the
John Gammon Peak District Crime Thrillers

Dad loved the farm, I always knew one day they would carry him out of there but not this soon.'

'I know, Mum.' John could feel the anger inside him - Lund had taken two of his family and he knew he had to get revenge.

A week passed. John had time off with his mother and slowly she started to take stock and John felt comfortable that she seemed ok. The funeral was to be the following Monday, April 13th at the family church.

John sat with his Mum on the Sunday before the funeral and she had the family album out looking at old pictures. 'Look how much Adam looks like your father, John.'

'Yes, he did, Mum, I thought I always looked like Uncle Graham - I have the same eyes and nose as your family, Mum.'

'Yes the Campbell's have strong genes - do you want a cup of tea?'

'Yes please, Mum.' Emily was making the tea and John could hear a whimpering coming from the kitchen. 'Mum, you ok?' There was no answer from Emily. ,John got up put the picture album on the coffee table and went into the farmhouse kitchen. Emily was crying. 'Mum, come here, it's going to be tough but I will be here for you.'

Sad Man
Second in the series of the
John Gammon Peak District Crime Thrillers

'I need to tell you something, son, and now seems the appropriate time. A couple of years after me and your Dad were wed, times were hard and we had just bought the farm that your Granddad left your Dad, Uncle Graham and their sister Irene along with quite a lot of money. We sunk everything into the farm. For one reason or another, financially, we were very poor as we tried to grow the business. Uncle Graham had a good job - he was Plant Manager at a steel works in Sheffield so the money wasn't needed straight away on his part.

'Uncle Graham offered to lend your Dad his share but your Dad would have none of it - he was very stubborn when he was younger just like our Adam. After about two years of a hard life, John, we hadn't had any children at this point, me and your Dad had a blazing row and I went to stop at my sisters in Grimley.'

'Oh, Aunty Evelyn.'

'Yes, John.'

'As I said, your Dad was very stubborn and I knew he would never chase after me. Anyway one night, there was a knock on the door and it was your Uncle Graham. He had been speaking to your Dad and had come to see if he could help get us back together - he had a house just outside Grimley so although your Dad never said, I think he had asked him to check on me.

'We decided to go for a drink, your Uncle Graham's life seemed so easy - not struggling for money and I was sick of the farm coming first.   Anyway, one thing led to another and before I knew it I was in bed with your Uncle Graham. To this day I regret it, John, please believe that.'

'Why are you telling me this?'

'Because, John, I fell pregnant and even though I went back to your Dad, some three weeks later I knew the baby wasn't your Dad's.'

'So where is the baby now?'

'It's you, John, your father or your Uncle Graham never knew.   They used to joke about the resemblance at family parties and I would just smile and act unassuming.'

'Mum, let me get this straight, my Dad is my Uncle Graham and he doesn't know?'

'That's correct, John, nobody knew me, and your Uncle Graham knew that what we had done was wrong and he took me straight back to my sisters that night. Your Dad was your proper Dad, Uncle Graham has never had any choice in the matter and your Dad loved you and was very proud of you, John.'

Sad Man
Second in the series of the
John Gammon Peak District Crime Thrillers

John's head was spinning, 'Why, Mum, why do you tell me now?'

'I thought this day would come, John, I never wanted to tell you while your father was alive - we never had a cross word after I came back. Your Dad was trying to build something for us all and he achieved - it he was the best husband any women could have wished for and we were very happy. I pushed the silly thing to the back of my mind and loved your Dad for all his worth. What you do with this information is your choice now, John.'

'Mum, I don't know but I am adult enough to know that you did the right thing by Dad and I thank you for that. Everyone makes mistakes in life, Mum, and you have paid I guess many times over. He will always be my Dad and that's the man I will bury tomorrow and the truth dies with Dad, Mum.'

'Son, I am so sorry for all of this.'

'Mum, it doesn't matter. Dad never knew and I will always be his son, so come on, make the tea.'

'Ok, John, what would I do without you?'

Friends and family started arriving at the farm for the funeral of Philip Gammon and the morning was blessed with bright sunshine. Roger Glazeback and his son Lestar were looking after the farm for

Sad Man
Second in the series of the
John Gammon Peak District Crime Thrillers

John's Mum and Roger said he would make the church for the service.

Uncle Graham and his wife Aunty Dinah were sat with Aunty Evelyn, Mum's sister. There was Shelley Etches and her husband and family, Denis and Clara from the Tow'd Man pub along with Doreen and Kevin from the Spinning Jenny in Swinster. Carol Lestar was stood talking to Bob and Cheryl, Steve Lineman and Jo were in conversation with Billy Sloverduck - John wasn't sure if that was his correct name but Billy and his father had been big friends and he always just called him Billy Sloverduck. John approached his Mum, 'The funeral director is here, Mum.' John had asked Billy Sloverduck, Steve Lineman, Denis, Kevin and one of the funeral directors to be the pallbearers alongside himself. They lifted Philip's coffin into the long black estate car and John climbed in the following car with his Mum.

'You ok, Mum?'

'Yes, John, I will be fine, you accept an age when these things are going to happen I guess. Are you still going to do that speech about your Dad, John?'

'Of course, Mum.'

They arrived at St Katherine's Church in Rowksly; it had not been that long since they buried Adam, which John knew would bring back memories for

Sad Man
Second in the series of the
John Gammon Peak District Crime Thrillers

his Mum. The pallbearers carried the coffin into the little church. The church was decorated with white and pink lilies - Philips favourite flower.

John placed a picture of Philip as a young man just a few years after his Mum and Dad were married - they had been on a day trip from the Spinning Jenny to Blackpool and somebody had taken a picture of Philip holding a pint of beer and candy floss. It was his Mums favourite picture.

The vicar of St Katherine's held the service. He relayed that sandwiches and refreshments would be served at the Spinning Jenny pub in Swinster and John and Emily would like all to attend and celebrate the life of Philip Gammon. It was now the turn of John and as he headed to the pulpit, he could see Janet Goslyarnee was in the congregation sat with Tony and Rita Sherriff, and Bob and Cheryl.

Arriving at the pulpit, John in his black Paul Smith suit with light blue shirt and black tie, was immaculate as usual. All his officers were in the congregation also and maybe for the first ever time, John felt nervous at public speaking.

His voice was shaky but he knew he had to do this for his Mum. 'My Dad, Philip Gammon - a man I looked up to, a man who never made me do anything but who knew when to push me. A great Dad to me and my brother, Adam, and a fantastic

Sad Man
Second in the series of the
John Gammon Peak District Crime Thrillers

husband to his wife and our Mum, Emily. I would like to read a small poem to you that I feel sums up my Dad as the person you all know:

If I could write a story,
It would be the greatest ever told.
Of a kind and loving father,
Who had a heart of gold.

If could write a million pages,
But still be unable to say, just how
Much I love and miss him,
Every single day

I will remember all he taught me,
I'm hurt but won't be sad.
Because he'll send me down the answers,
And he'll always be MY DAD.'

John climbed down from the pulpit, stopping for a second to place his hand on Philip's coffin and to wipe a tear from his eye. Emily was being comforted by her sister.

Eventually after the burial of Philip Gammon, the congregation gathered at the Spinning Jenny in Swinster. Doreen put a buffet on for Emily and would not accept payment for it - they had been friends for a long time.

Sad Man
Second in the series of the
John Gammon Peak District Crime Thrillers

Carol Lestar gave John a big hug and stated how sorry she was so soon after losing Adam. The pub was packed - John never realised how popular Philip was. He had been a keen footballer and cricketer and had been a big member of Hittington Dale Tug of War teams over many years. Their biggest rivals from Micklock were represented by a dozen members.

The funeral and wake went without too much upset but by 10pm both John and Emily were ready to call it a day. There were only the big drinkers left around the bar so Emily and John thanked Doreen and Kevin for their kindness and they slipped away. John told his mother he would stay with her a couple of nights just until she felt a bit better.

The case had not moved much further on while John's time had been taken up with his loss and John had felt more inclined to try and get something on Lund but he knew that was unprofessional and that his time would come.

Steve and Jo's engagement party had soon come around - he was now back in his cottage but phoning his Mum every day. Roger Glazeback and his son were running the farm for his Mum so he knew she would be ok. John decided to go to Bixton to see if he could get an engagement present for Jo and Steve.

Sad Man
Second in the series of the
John Gammon Peak District Crime Thrillers

He parked his jaguar at the top of the hill and walked down to the shopping mall in Bixton. Bixton had been a Victorian Spa town where the poorly rich people came to take the spa waters which they believed would make them better.

John spotted a wine decanter and six wine goblets in Dartington cut glass which he thought would go with Jo's mansion. John bought the present and had it wrapped by the assistant who also supplied an engagement card. *That was simple,* John thought as he left the shop. Walking across the street, he thought he recognised a guy standing by a taxi. 'Hey, Mr Reynolds, he shouted.' The guy looked up and quickly jumped in the taxi and signalled for the driver to move on. *Damn,* Gammon thought. He quickly phoned Inspector Evans and explained what he had seen and gave Evans the registration number of the taxi to follow up.

'I will meet you at the station tomorrow morning at 10.00am for an update inspector.'

'Ok, Evans.' John got to his car; he was about to set off when his phone rang - it was Sergeant Carl Milton. 'What do you want, Milton?'

'To be honest, Sir, a stiff brandy would not go a miss - could you meet me somewhere?'

Sad Man
Second in the series of the
John Gammon Peak District Crime Thrillers

'I'll meet you at the Wobbly Man in Toad Holes if you like.'

'How long, Sir?'

'Ten minutes.'

'Ok, Sir.'

When Gammon arrived at the Wobbly Man, Carl was already there sat at a small table. 'I got you a pint, Sir.'

'Thanks, Carl, now what's the problem?'

'Well to be honest, it's not a problem but I would like your advice.'

'Ok, Carl, what is it?'

'You know my girlfriend Beth who died after the shooting at the junior school? Well, they read the will today and me, Joni Horalek and Beth's brother Ben have been left £687,000.00 pounds each by Beth.'

'Wow, now that is a lot of money, Carl.'

'It is, Sir, but the first thing that ran through my mind is what could I spend that kind of money on that would always remind me of Beth.'

'Beth had been a high-flying banker in London, Carl, am I correct?'

Sad Man
Second in the series of the
John Gammon Peak District Crime Thrillers

'Yes, Sir.'

'I think I met her once at a big charity do down there but she was Victoria Wagers then.'

'Well, it's a long story but let's just say the poor girl went through hell for no reason other than these people wanted money out of her bank.

'The cottage we shared, I am thinking of asking Rita Butts if I could buy it as a legacy to Beth, Sir.'

'I like the idea, Carl, but I would wait a few months until your heads is cleared before making such a big decision.'

Just then Joni Horalek came in, she had been crying so Carl got up and comforted her. 'Please join us, Joni, this is Superintendent Gammon, my boss at Bixton.'

'Pleased to meet you, Superintendent Gammon.'

'Please call me, John, I am not on duty.'

'Ok, John it is. I am so in shock about what Beth did, John.'

'She sounds like she was one hell of a person - you were both lucky to have known her. Listen, please don't think I am being funny but I am going to an engagement party tonight so I have a few things I need to do.'

Sad Man
Second in the series of the
John Gammon Peak District Crime Thrillers

'That's odd, we were going to one at Up the Steps Maggie's.'

'Steve Lineman and Jo Wickets?'

'Yes, now that is a coincidence! How do you know Jo and Steve?'

'Carl doesn't actually but I do, me and Jo used to play together if she ever came to see her aunty when we were little so we kept in touch. Carl is going to keep me company tonight.'

'Ok, you two, then I'll see you there tonight.'

'You surely will,' Joni said and gave Gammon that smile that meant she hoped so.

'Stop fraternising with my boss, Horalek.'

'He is flippin' gorgeous - you better make yourself scarce tonight, Carlos, I am on the pull,' and she laughed.

John arrived back at the cottage and phoned his Mum. 'Hi, Mum how are you today?'

'Not bad, John, Roger and his son have been a massive help but I think I need to decide what I want to do with the farm.'

'Mum, don't do anything for six months - see how it plays out first or you may regret it.' The conversation carried on for possibly fifteen minutes

Sad Man
Second in the series of the
John Gammon Peak District Crime Thrillers

then John told his Mum he was going to get ready for Steve and Jo's party.

It was 8.15pm when the taxi pulled up to take John to the engagement party at Up the Steps Maggie's. John gave the instruction to the taxi driver and they set off. 'I was sorry to hear that your brother died in vain and that the nutter Lund is still roaming free, pal.'

'Thank you but it's been a bad time for my family so I would prefer not to talk about it.'

'No problem, pal,' said the driver. They sat in silence for the rest of the journey.

They arrived at the party at 8.35pm and John could hear the disco belting out some music. There was a chill in the air as he walked into the pub. Jo met John and thanked him for coming and he handed Jo his present and spoke with Steve. 'Good turnout, quite few here, mate.'

'Well, we were only going to have a small party then you know how it goes, you remember somebody you missed off the list then they have a partner, and so it goes...'

Carl came up and shook John's hand, 'Good to see you, Sir.'

'John, Carl, call me John when we are off duty.'

Sad Man
Second in the series of the
John Gammon Peak District Crime Thrillers

'Hello, handsome one, fancy a dance?'

'Excuse me, I will take Joni away.'

'No you won't, Carl, this is one stunning lady. Yes, I will have a dance, Joni.' On the dance floor, Joni was wearing a green dress with no back, her hair best described as a short Tina Turner cut. They danced for three songs; Off the Wall by Michael Jackson, Cool for Cats by Squeeze and Danni by Blondie. By this time, most of the guests had arrived and Steve decided on a speech. 'Ladies and Gentlemen, family and friends, may I first of all thank you for coming - I know some of you have travelled long distances to be here and me and Jo really appreciate that. I would just like to thank you again and please have a great night because I know we will.'

From the back John could hear Tony Sherriff shouting 'more' as were Lairy Bob and Carol Lestar. Steve handed the microphone to the DJ and they danced to Islands In The Stream By Kenny and Dolly - *very apt*, thought John. By 10.00pm Carl was dancing with Carol Lestar and Joni had snared John in a corner deep in conversation.

They were close to the kissing stage when John's phone rang - it was Inspector Evans. 'Sir, there has been another victim, only this time she is dead.' John made his excuses to Joni and said he would call in the Wobbly Man to see her and arrange a night out. He explained to Steve and Jo, and Steve gave him the car keys to his Range Rover.

'I will drop it off tomorrow, Steve.'

'No problem, you ok to drive?'

'Yeah only had two pints.'

'Too busy talking to Joni, hey, John?'

'Guess so, Jo...'

Evans had told Gammon that the victim was not that far from Micklock moor and he would meet him by the sign for Dilley Dale before you entered Micklock moor. Evans was already waiting for Gammon when he arrived. It was now just after 11.20pm and the moor looked a desolate place; the sky was dull and hung over the landscape like a grey sea of mist.

'Evening, Sir.'

'Yes, good evening, inspector, what have we got?'

'Forensics are taking swabs from her body - they say she died approximately at 9.45pm. When we turned the body over she had scratch marks all up her arm so we're pretty sure it's the same guy who attacked the other two. One strange thing, Sir, it looks like she tried to scratch a name in the mud.'

Sad Man
Second in the series of the
John Gammon Peak District Crime Thrillers

'What was the name?'

'Well, it was hard to see but I would have said 'Matt'. She only got three letters done though 'MAT'.'

'It could be anything, Evans.'

'I know, Sir, but I thought I better tell you.'

'What about next of kin?'

'I have an address for her parents, Sir.'

'Ok, Evans, let's go and do the dirty bit of the job.'

Gammon and Evans drove to Bonne Nuir in Dilley Dale; as they drove up the long driveway the house was stunning, possibly an eight bedroomed house with a big sweeping drive. They walked up to the tall oak door with a fancy brass lion's head for a knocker on it, Gammon knocked once and a light came on. A man in his early sixties with grey hair, dressed in his pyjamas and a bed robe walked up the hall. 'Can I help you?' he shouted through the glass.

'Superintendent Gammon and Inspector Evans, Bixton Police, Sir, could we have a word please?' They showed their warrant cards and just as the man was opening his door a lady, again maybe mid fifties, with long blonde hair joined him.

'What's the problem, officers?'

Sad Man
Second in the series of the
John Gammon Peak District Crime Thrillers

'Could we come in?'

'Sure, would you like a coffee?'

'Excuse my attire, I am waiting for my daughter to come home and my wife was upstairs reading. Neither of us sleeps until Suzy gets home - we had her quite late in life - we thought our chance had gone then our beautiful daughter came along. Sorry officers, I suppose you are here about the robbery down the road the other night - we did give statements and we didn't see anything else.'

'Please sit down, Mr Warner, Mrs Warner.'

'Oh call me Thomas, and my wife is Lena.'

'Thomas, Lena, I am very sorry, but I have bad news for you. Your daughter was murdered tonight.' Mrs Warner let out a scream and threw her head into her hands. Mr Warner just went pale and shook his head.

Then the blame started. Mrs Warner said, 'If you had not been going to that stupid bridge party, you could have picked Suzy up,' and she cried some more.

'We are very sorry for your loss, could you tell me something of Suzy's whereabouts tonight? Or do you want to wait and we will call back in the morning?'

Sad Man
Second in the series of the
John Gammon Peak District Crime Thrillers

'I'm not sure where they were going.'

'They, Mr Warner?'

'Yes, Suzy and her boyfriend, Mark.'

'Can you give me a full name and address for Mark?'

By now Mrs Warner had composed herself. 'His full name is Mark Anthony, his father is a professor at Derby University in Roman History and Science, hence the Mark Anthony.'

'What is the surname?'

'Tink, Mr Gammon.' John shot a knowing glance across to Inspector Evans. 'They live at The Cherries on Guillet Lane in Swinster, Mr Gammon.'

'Do you need anybody to stay with you tonight?'

'No, we will be fine, Superintendent, when can we see Suzy?'

'You will have to formerly identify the body tomorrow - I will call you, if I could just have your number?' Mr Warner gave Gammon a business card with 'Warner Brothers Jewellers' written on it. 'Ok, Mr Warner, I will call you both tomorrow.'

When they got outside, Evans could not hold his disbelief, 'So that is Mr Warner of Warner Brothers jewellers? He is a 'Sir' - I believe he makes all the

Sad Man
Second in the series of the
John Gammon Peak District Crime Thrillers

Royal family's jewellery - I only know this because my Mum would always say to my Dad 'hell will freeze over before you can afford to buy me a ring from Warner's."

'Very interesting, Evans.'

The ride after that was quite silent. Gammon was thinking about the letters Suzy had scrawled in the mud - *were they her boyfriend's initials?* They pulled up outside yet another big house and walked up the drive where there was a Porsche and a Mercedes with a personalised number plate on the Porsche reading T 1NK.

Just as Gammon was about to ring the doorbell, he suddenly remembered that one of the victim's friends was called Suzy Warner and she was the one the taxi driver was hitting on. The doorbell made a sound like a church bell. All the lights were on downstairs; it was 2am when a young man came to the door. 'Could we speak to Mark Anthony?' They both showed their warrant cards. The guy bolted past them and started running. There was no way Evans could catch him so Gammon told him to stay at the house in case Mr and Mrs Tink came down. Gammon was a former Derbyshire four hundred metre runner so was no slouch when chasing somebody but the guy was quick and after a third of mile he had gone, so Gammon walked back to the house.

Sad Man
Second in the series of the
John Gammon Peak District Crime Thrillers

As he approached the drive he could see that a heated discussion was taking place on the porch with Evans and a man and woman he assumed to be Mr and Mrs Tink. 'What's the problem, Evans?'

'Mr Tink is saying he will call his lawyer and that his son wasn't driving the Porsche and that he had been home all night.'

'Is he really?' said Gammon. 'May we come in, Mr Tink? Can I explain the situation to you - we are not here about an accident in your Porsche, although I will be looking into that, we are here to ask your son some questions about a murder case. From where I am standing, it doesn't look good for him now that he has run off. Evans, I want a helicopter up looking for him and as many squad cars as possible.

'Now, Mr Tink, were you driving the Porsche?'

'No, it was Mark Anthony, he was going out with his new girlfriend Lucy or Suzy or something and apparently he hit a road work sign which crushed the wing and scraped the paintwork - he would be showing off I don't doubt.'

'Why do you think your son ran off when he saw us, Mr Tink?'

'I don't know, officer.'

Sad Man
Second in the series of the
John Gammon Peak District Crime Thrillers

'Well let's hope he isn't a silly boy and he hands himself in. While we are here, do you mind if we have a look in his room?'

'I'm not sure about that - we aren't allowed in his room.'

'Mr Tink, this is a murder investigation - the young lady your son was seeing was murdered tonight.'

Mrs Tink fell back on the settee, 'Mark Anthony would not do anything like that.'

'Go ahead, officers, it's the first bedroom at the top of the stairs.'

'Thank you, Mr Tink.' Evans and Gammon climbed the sweeping staircase - the house was like something out of Dallas, there was serious money being made somewhere. They opened the door and it was like any teenager's bedroom - clothes everywhere, 42" Plasma TV on the wall and an X Box connected to it.

On the walls were poster of Nirvana, Miley Cyrus and the like. Evans started looking through the bedside cabinet drawers. 'Look what I have found, Sir, a small bag of happy dust, I think.'

Gammon placed a very small amount on his little finger and rubbed it on his gum. 'That's cocaine, Inspector, bag it up. This DVD collection is a bit on the weird side - look at this one, Evans: The Night I

Sad Man
Second in the series of the
John Gammon Peak District Crime Thrillers

Became a Serial Killer and another I Will Force Myself on You. Bag these up as well, Evans for when we talk to this piece of trash.'

'Sir, I have found a packet of razor blades - didn't the first two victims say this guy's coat had razor blades or barbed wire or something stitched into it?'

'Bag them as well, Evans. Arrange for a full house search from top to bottom.'

'Will do, Sir.'

'There's not much more we can do here, Evans, until they catch him, so call it a night and I will see you in the morning.'

'Oh, Sir, it's Sunday tomorrow.'

'I know, Evans.'

'Well, I always take my Mum to Aunty Maria's in Stoke on a Sunday then we go to church.'

'Ok, Evans, I will see you Monday, give Milton a call and tell him to be in work in the morning at 10am.'

'Will do, Sir.'

Gammon drove home arriving at the cottage around 2.10am; it was a full moon and the little cottage was bathed in moonlight. Gammon's mind was racing so he decided to sit by the log burner and have a glass of his ten-year-old Malt Whisky that Vicky had

Sad Man
Second in the series of the
John Gammon Peak District Crime Thrillers

bought him when they were together. A gloom descended on his being. One glass was never going to be enough and he started to struggle with the events that had happened in his life of late. Adam dead, his Dad dead, his marriage over, his friendship with Jeanette at an all time low... Vicky gone and he knew he could never have that relationship again. Before John knew where he was it was 5.30am and he woke cold in the armchair, the fire gone out and the bottle of malt whisky empty lying on the floor.

John climbed the stairs feeling the effects of the whisky and clambered into bed. In no time he was fast asleep. It was 9.30am when the loud ring on his mobile woke him - it was his Mum. 'Hi John, I wondered if you wanted to come for Sunday lunch today?'

'Mum, I am so sorry, but I have to work.'

'No problem, son, are you ok?'

'Just had a late night at work, Mum.'

'Oh I thought you were going to Steve Lineman's party?'

'I did, but I am afraid I was called away for work, Mum.'

Sad Man
Second in the series of the
John Gammon Peak District Crime Thrillers

'Well you go careful, John, work will be there long after you are gone, that's what I used to tell your Dad - not that he listened though.'

'Ok, Mum, well I better go - I need to get into work.'

John showered and dressed, he felt like there was an army of workmen with hammers banging in his head. He would normally have called at the greasy spoon on the way in but thought better with the way he was feeling.

It was 10.15am when he arrived at Bixton police station and Sergeant Carl Milton was already waiting. 'Morning, Sir.'

'Morning, Sergeant, have we got a search warrant for the Tink house?'

'Yes, Sir, Scooper and Smarty are on the way to the house now with a search team.'

'Ok, keep me informed.' Gammon turned round to go to his office when the police station doors flung open and two constables had Mark Anthony Tink in cuffs. He looked very dishevelled. 'Well well nice to see you, Mr Tink. Put him in interview room one.

'Come on, Milton, I am going to enjoy this one.' Carl put the interview tape on and introduced everyone in the room to the tape. 'Ok, Mr Tink, are we going to get some cooperation with your situation or are you just going to be a silly boy? Do you want legal representation?'

'I haven't done anything.'

'I will ask you one more time - do you want legal representation, Mr Tink?'

'No.'

'Ok, for the tape, you are Mark Anthony Tink is that correct?'

'Yes.'

'Were you seeing Miss Suzy Warner, Mark? Ok if I call you Mark?'

'Yes, no problem.'

'So in answer to my question...'

'Yes, I had been seeing Suzy for about three months.'

'Would you say you had a volatile relationship?'

'Not really, we only argued maybe twice.'

'What were the arguments about Mark?'

'Well Suzy could be a bit flirty and I got jealous one night, she was playing up to some rugby lads in the bar.'

Sad Man
Second in the series of the
John Gammon Peak District Crime Thrillers

'Did you get violent with Suzy, Mark?'

'No never, I would not, I am not violent.'

'So just run over last night - you picked Suzy up, then what?'

'We drove around for a while and Suzy wanted to go clubbing. I didn't want to so we argued and I stopped the car, she got out of the car and said she would walk to the club in Micklock. I was annoyed so I stormed off. Because the car was fast I nearly lost it on a bend and I clipped a 'men at work' sign - you know, those metal triangle things they have near manhole covers. I was going to go back to make sure Suzy was ok but when I saw the damage to my Dad's car I thought I would be better taking it home and anyway I was still annoyed with Suzy. She was such a party animal and I didn't always feel like it.'

'Are you a drugs user, Mark?'

'No, why?'

Sergeant Milton produced the bag of cocaine. 'This was found in your bedroom at your house.'

'It's not mine - it was Suzy's.'

'Well isn't that handy? Suzy can't speak for herself.'

Sad Man
Second in the series of the
John Gammon Peak District Crime Thrillers

'Look, I will take a drugs test, anything, I am telling you - it wasn't mine.'

'I will take you up on that, Mark. Arrange that please, Sergeant Milton, also I want Suzy Warner's body checked for illegal substances, Sergeant.'

'Yes, Sir.'

'Now, Mark, you are telling us that Suzy was a drug user and she was flirty with all the guys.'

'Yes.'

'So tell me - why you would want to be with somebody like that?'

'Well the flirting was annoying but she was very pretty with a good figure and she liked the attention. The drug thing I didn't know she was using until two nights ago - she was at our house and we were playing records in my bedroom when she produced the bag of cocaine from her handbag. She used some and tried to get me to but I wouldn't. She asked me if I would store it for her as her Mum went in her bedroom whereas my parents didn't so I agreed. I know it was wrong but she could be very persuasive.'

'Mark, I possibly believe you on this but let me put a scenario to you. I think you argued and she got out of the car, you were annoyed so you drove after her, she stepped out in front of the car and you hit her - what do you reckon to that?'

'I did not. I have told you the truth.'

'Well for now, I am charging you with possession of a Class A drug, interview ended. Sergeants, take him to the custody please.'

Gammon walked across to Sergeant Hanney, 'What is the current position on Mr Reynolds? Have we contacted the Northumbria police, Sergeant?'

'Yes, that was done yesterday - they have an address for Mr Reynolds - they believe it may be his mother's house so they are going round today. I am expecting an answer sometime today.'

'Ok, Sergeant, I am calling it a day. If you hear anything, give me a call on my mobile.'

'Will do, Sir.' Gammon walked across the car park to his Jaguar. It was now Sunday afternoon and he was unsure what to do so he decided to drive down to the Wobbly Man and see if Joni was working. Through the winding roads leading from Bixton to Toad holes, Gammon reflected. Did he need the hassle of another girlfriend? Had he outstayed his welcome? He wanted to get back to London but was now trapped with his father having died. There

Sad Man
Second in the series of the
John Gammon Peak District Crime Thrillers

was also the small matter of Brian Lund and he was determined to sort him out.

He arrived at the Wobbly Man and the small breeze was making the Wobbly Man sign swing, and being an old sign, it creaked. Toad Holes was a nice little village - a lot of the locals still lived there although there had been a massive influx of people from down south who could afford the sky-high prices the houses were fetching in Toad Holes.

Gammon parked his car at the side of the pub and entered through the side door. He could see Joni from a distance working at the bar. The pub was quite full, it was well known for its Sunday lunches and on a Sunday afternoon they had a local guy with his guitar singing from 4pm until 8 pm. Sultry Simon the locals called him because he had this habit of curling his lip Elvis-like while he sang, although to be fair, he was quite good.

'Hi, John,' Joni beamed. 'Didn't expect to see you so soon.'

'I had to work this morning, Joni.'

'Yeah shame you had to leave last night. What are you drinking?'

'I'll try a pint of City Slicker please.'

'Very apt, John,' and she laughed. Joni was a pretty girl, John thought, but he wondered why she wasn't with anyone - he guessed she was very picky when it came to men.

'There you go, John.'

'Thanks, do you fancy having a drink Wednesday night?'

'Oh John, I can't, I go to Pilates on Wednesdays - what about Thursday night?'

'Fine by me, Joni, where do you live?'

'Do you know where Beth lived, Carl's girlfriend, at Mrs Butt's cottage?'

'Yes.'

'Well, I live at the next cottage going up the hill - it's called Surprise View Cottage.'

'Ok, Joni, I will pick you up at 7.15pm and we can go for a meal at the Spinning Jenny - I like their food better than at the Tow'd Man. Look forward to it.' John left the bar with Joni being busy and sat round the corner near the fire.

He was just about to finish his pint when two big guys came in looking like something you see on WWF. The two big guys pushed their way to the bar making like a walkway and next in was Brian Lund with girl of about twenty seven; she looked like something out of a Vogue magazine. John had all on controlling his temper, he got up and walked over to Lund and the two big guys immediately stood shoulder to shoulder with him.

Lund got right up in John's face. 'Well, surprise, surprise, its prostitute user's brother, the little detective, how are you, Gammon?'

'Well, scumbag,' he retorted, 'I am better than you will be when I finish with you.'

'Is that a threat, Gammon? Did you hear that people? Harassment from a serving officer?'

'It's not a threat,' Gammon said, 'It's a promise,' and he walked out.

The big guys were about to go out but Lund stopped them, 'Leave it, our time will come, lads. Now then, pretty barmaid, what can you do for me today?'

'I can bar you for causing problems in the pub.'

Lund laughed, 'You stupid girl, don't you know who I am?'

'Oh yes, I know who you are.' The locals all stood up in defence of Joni as she was a well-liked girl.

'Looks like the village idiots are out in force today, lads, let's find another pub.' As they turned to go, Lund drew a line across his throat with his finger to Joni in a cutting motion. 'Hope to see you soon barmaid...'

Sad Man
Second in the series of the
John Gammon Peak District Crime Thrillers

When they left the pub, Joni was shaking. 'That was very brave of you, Joni.'

'I realise that now, Bomber.' Bomber was a regular in the Wobbly Man; word had it he had been in the SAS - he never spoke about it but nobody crossed Bomber. 'Our country needs more people like you, Joni.' Rick Hieb the landlord poured Joni a large brandy and told her to sit down.

Gammon had left the pub and gone to the Spinning Jenny to book his and Joni's table for Thursday night he - had no idea what had happened in the Wobbly Man. He booked the table with Doreen and ordered a pint of Hissing Sid from Kev. He sat with Carol Lestar. 'Are you ok, John?' John started to tell Carol about Brian Lund when the door opened and Lund and his party came in.

Kev took one look at Lund and just said, 'Out!'

'What have I done, landlord?'

'You are a murdering scumbag - one of my best friends died two week ago after seeing your face on the TV, now get out of my pub.' At this one of the big protection guys lifted Kev by the throat. Gammon flew out of his chair and with one swipe at the side of the big guy's neck he dropped like a bag of cement. The second big guy squared up to Gammon. 'Son, I would think long and hard about this.' No sooner had Gammon got the words out of his mouth had Doreen heard the commotion and she hit the big guy with a full bottle of whisky over the head.

She then looked at Lund, 'Do you want some, you scumbag?'

Lund looked at her, turned to the model holding onto his arm and started to walk out. As he approached the low-beamed door he turned round and said, 'Hopefully we will meet again on different terms, Madam.'

Gammon had already called for back up. The officers arrived and took the two big guys away. 'Book them for causing an affray.' They duly took the big guys away in handcuffs. Kev was having a large brandy and trying to adjust his red dickie bow.

Doreen wasn't bothered. 'They don't scare me, John, they are just low lifes.'

'Thanks to both of you for supporting me and my family.'

'John, your father was a very dear friend of mine and there was no way that scumbag was having a drink in my pub.'

'Thanks, Kev,' and John returned to his seat with Carol Lestar.

Sad Man
Second in the series of the
John Gammon Peak District Crime Thrillers

'Flippin' heck, John, where did you learn to drop such a big guy like that with one blow?'

'I did a lot of undercover work when I was in London, Carol, and you have to be fully aware of the danger you may be in.'

'Well that was impressive - a Sunday drink with James Bond - wait until I put that on Facebook,' and she laughed.

Bob and Cheryl arrived, 'What happened, Kev? We saw all the blue lights flashing and heard the Sirens.'

'It's a long story, Cheryl. John will tell you - he is sat with Carol round the corner.'

Cheryl went off to talk to John while Bob got the drinks. 'So how are you, cutie pie?'

'Oh don't you start, Doreen, everyone is calling me that now since the other night.'

'So which do you prefer - Lairy Bob, Pants on Your Head Bob or Cutie pie, Bob? Only I need something to put on the posters for next week's show.'

'Just stick with Pants on Your Head Bob,' and he took his drinks quickly away from the bar.

Doreen chuckled, 'First time I have seen Bob lost for words, Kev.'

Sad Man
Second in the series of the
John Gammon Peak District Crime Thrillers

'Yeah me too, Doreen.'

At 4pm, as was the normal, Doreen came out with a big tray of roast potatoes for the locals and hot beef cobs. 'Tuck in,' she said. 'We have a guy who plays guitar coming at 5pm - he is a mate of Kev's, they used to work together down the mine years ago before we took the Spinning Jenny.'

'Can I tell a few jokes then as well, Doreen?'

'Cutie Pie...' the words only just came out of her mouth and she stopped herself, 'I mean, Bob, of cause you can.'

'Do you have to, Bob?'

'I have some cracking new material, Cheryl, I need to try it out. Tell me what you think of this one:

"My wife is having twins, Paddy. I'm going on a business trip soon and if she gives birth while I'm away, I want you dear brother, to name the kids," says Mick.
"It'll be an honour to do that for you, Mick," says Paddy.
A month later Paddy calls Mick.
"Hello, Mick, your wife's given birth to a boy and a girl, they're beautiful," says Paddy.
"That's wonderful, Paddy, what did you call them?" says Mick.
"I called the girl Denise," says Paddy.

Sad Man
Second in the series of the
John Gammon Peak District Crime Thrillers

"Great, like that name!"
"And what did you call the boy?"
"I called the boy De-nephew.'"

'That's dreadful, Bob, don't give up your day job,' Carol shouted.
The friend of Kev's arrived; he looked a bit like Roy Orbison, he had black hair clearly dyed and wore the Orbison sunglasses. Kev introduced the guy. 'Ladies and Gentlemen, I would like you to give a big hand for a very old friend of mine - we worked down the pit too many years ago to remember. Please give a big hand to Bobbie Tilley.'

Bobbie got straight on with his first song Pretty Woman, an Orbison classic. 'He is very good don't you think, Carol?'

'Very impressed, Kev, how come he hasn't been before?'

'He lives in Tenerife so is always booked up all year round, they have a lot of these types of acts over there. When he left the pit he wasn't married and used to always be singing so he took his chance and went out to Tenerife, it must be thirty years ago now. He is back at the moment, his Mum passed away so he is sorting her estate out and called me out of the blue.'

Sad Man
Second in the series of the
John Gammon Peak District Crime Thrillers

'Glad he did, Kev, he is brilliant.

Steve and Jo walked in. 'You're late, Lineman,' shouted Carol Lestar.
'Don't you start, gobby.'
At this, Jo smacked Steve on his arm, 'There's no need for that, Steve, Carol was only having a bit of fun.'

'Sorry, Carol, let me get you a drink.'

'Never turn down a drink, Steve!'

'Thought that, Carol.' Gammon got up to get a round in and get a drink for Steve and Jo.

'I'll get these, John.'

'Are you sure, it's a big round?'

'Yes, no problem, what is everyone drinking?'

'Bob is on Pedigree, Cheryl is drinking rum and coke, I'll have a pint of Hissing Sid, and Carol is drinking double vodka and diet coke.'

'Hey, if it's not Piggy and Offside, the bloody terrible twins, how are you both?'

Sad Man
Second in the series of the
John Gammon Peak District Crime Thrillers

'Albert Coors, as I live and breathe, what the hell are you doing up here? Thought you had moved to York.'

'Yeah we did, Steve, we are visiting the wife's uncle - remember Slim Radford?'

'Yeah he was three years above us at school - big guy.'

'That's the one, well he is my wife, Helen's uncle. He had a motorbike accident a few month ago, lucky to be alive really but he has made it and he came out of hospital this week so she wanted to get him settled in. His wife died when she was quite young so they have no kids and he has always looked on Helen as his daughter. So what about you two? I heard about Adam, very sorry for your loss, John. Also heard you were a top cop now.'

I don't know about that, Bert, we just lost my Dad also. Think everything piled up on him.'

'Oh, John, I'm sorry, I didn't know Phil had passed on. What about you, Steve?'

'Well I left the merchant navy and met the love of my life - she is over there.'

'Which one? Not the slim, good-looking blonde?'

'Yeah.'

Sad Man
Second in the series of the
John Gammon Peak District Crime Thrillers

'Bloody hell, Offside, you did well there.'

'It gets better, Bert, she is flippin' loaded. Steve is busy doing her mansion up.'

'He always was a jammy buggar, wasn't he, John?'

'Sure was, Bert.'

'Right, lads, better make a move, think the wife wants to get back. Great to see you both.'

'You too, Bert.'

'How long is it since you last saw Albert Coors, John?'

'It must be at least fifteen years, Steve.'

'Must be about the same for me.'

'Remember at school when he set the bike shed on fire smoking and he blamed you, Steve.'

'Yeah, I flippin' do remember - I got six whacks with that bloody cane off Billy Henderson, he was a proper sadist him, he actually enjoyed giving anyone pain!'

'Tell you what, John, this Bobby Tilly is a good singer - you would think it was Roy Orbison up there.'

Sad Man
Second in the series of the
John Gammon Peak District Crime Thrillers

'Don't think Bob is too impressed, he can't wait for his break to come so he can get up and tell a few jokes, Steve.'

The night was a great success. Jo and Steve gave John a lift home from the Spinning Jenny as she hadn't been drinking that night. They pulled up at John's little cottage. 'Do you fancy a nightcap, you two?'

'We're fine, John, thanks - heavy day tomorrow.'

'Ok well, thanks for the lift. I'll try and get up to see you both next week to see how the renovations are going.'

'Ok, that would be nice, John, goodnight.' John closed the car door and made his way to the front door of the cottage. John stood for a moment as Jo's car disappeared up the drive. It was a beautiful full moon - there were stars everywhere and he just knew his Dad and brother were looking down on him.

Monday morning back at the station in Bixton, Gammon called a meeting to discuss the case currently on going. The incident room was a shabby looking room, most of the detectives had a desk in there. The window had shabby blinds on them and the place clearly had not had a lick of paint in a long time. Gammon stood by the white

Sad Man
Second in the series of the
John Gammon Peak District Crime Thrillers

flip chart. 'Ok, gather round everyone.' They all huddled to the front. 'Ok, current cases needing attention. Number one, where are we on the spate of robberies in Bixton at the Nightingale Housing Complex?'

'Two men arrested, Sir.'

'Have we got the evidence Sergeant Bannon?'

'Yes, Sir, myself and PC Di Trimble are the arresting officers and they were caught red handed by a member of the public.'

'Great Bannon, one less to worry about. Ok, Case Two - cock fighting at Berry's farm in Hittington and news on that.'

'Yes, Sir, apparently the farm was rented for the weekend by a Mr Sawledge from Cuthberts estate agents. The guy had given a false name but Mr Kruger from the estate agents took his number plate down and that's how we traced him - he was arrested yesterday by Di Trimble and myself, Sir.'

'Great, well done, you two. Case three - as you know, one very close to my thoughts - Brian Lund and the Drovers arms in Derby.'

'I spent the weekend there, Sir, nothing too dramatic going on. There was a guy selling weed but Lund and his cronies only came in once.'

Sad Man
Second in the series of the
John Gammon Peak District Crime Thrillers

'Ok, Scooper, you and Dave Smarty spend the rest of the week seeing what you can dig up. Ok, the big one - where are we with the rape and what has now turned into a murder case?'

'We have still been unable to locate James Reynolds - he had been at his mother's house but we just missed him, his picture has been circulated to all police forces. Mark Anthony Tink has been released but I don't want him counting out of our investigations. The taxi driver Cristos Minolis I believe is a good suspect, I may have some ideas about what we do with him - I will share in a few days.'

'Ok, Sergeant Milton, you come with me, I have some nagging doubts about the rape/murder case.'

'Where are we going, Sir?'

'I think it's a bit strange that Dana Braint was raped in a ploughed field on Micklock Moor and Milan Peterson was also raped on Micklock Moor. The body of Suzy Warner was also found near Micklock Moor. I want to go and have another talk to Miss Alison.'

Sergeant Milton drove the police car to Micklock Moor. 'Who is this lady, Sir?'

Sad Man
Second in the series of the
John Gammon Peak District Crime Thrillers

'Well, apparently, she is the last surviving heir to a Hydro dynasty - she is very strange, almost ignorant you would say and I think a recluse.'

They drove up the drive to Miss Alison's mansion. The mansion was in need of some serious repairs, there was ivy clinging to all the exterior walls and some of the ivy covered the upstairs windows. The gardens were surprisingly neat and tidy with rhododendron bushes of all colours lining the drive. The lawns were immaculate and looked like they had just been cut. As Gammon and Milton got out of the car they could hear raised voices coming from the back of the house. As they approached down the side of the house, a quite tall guy with a woolly hat on, grey overalls and wellington boots was coming the other way. He looked at Gammon and just said, 'Bloody silly old bat.'

'Excuse me, Sir, but who are you?'

'Eric Stein, head gardener, why who's asking?' Gammon flashed his warrant card Superintendent John Gammon Bixton Police. 'What do you want from me?'

'Just a quick word, Sir. Do you work here fulltime?'

'No, I do three and a half days a week here and I work two days as a pot washer and kitchen hand at Up the Steps Maggie's pub.'

Sad Man
Second in the series of the
John Gammon Peak District Crime Thrillers

'Are you local?'

'I live in the old poor house in Swinster.'

'Miss Alison - does she live here alone do you know?'

'Don't know, don't care, she is bloody batty anyway. I have heard her speaking to somebody but have never seen anyone in the five years I've worked here. Think she talks to herself.'

'Ok, Mr Stein, thanks for your help.'
'What has the old buggar done anyway?'

'Nothing as far as we are aware but she lives close to the reported rapes so we have to look at everything.'

'Right, I better get on, she wants the outside toilet fixing - its overflowing and apparently keeps her awake at night!'

Gammon and Milton reached the back kitchen door and startled Miss Alison as she was putting rubbish in the bin. 'What do you want again?'

'Miss Alison, I would just like to ask you a few more questions about the other night - can we come in?'

'No, ask what you want here.'

Sad Man
Second in the series of the
John Gammon Peak District Crime Thrillers

'Ok, Miss Alison, if you insist. Have you seen anybody suspicious hanging around the area?'

'No.'

'Do you live alone?'

'Yes.'

'Your gardener, Mr Stein, said he has heard you talking to somebody - is that correct?'

'I must have had a quiz on the radio and was shouting out the answers.'

'So you live alone?'

'Yes.'

'That must be quite lonely.'

'No, I like my own company, I am only waiting to die anyway.'

'I guess we are all in that queue, Miss Alison. Your gardener - Mr Stein, how long has he worked for you?'

'About five years.'

'Does he ever come in your house, say for a cup of tea?'

Sad Man
Second in the series of the
John Gammon Peak District Crime Thrillers

'No, I don't encourage the lower classes, he is the gardener and he has a shed where he can take lunch. I don't supply tea, I'm not a cafe.

'Ok, Miss Alison, please let me know if you think of anything that may be of help to us. This is my card.' Miss Alison took the card and placed it in her small clutch bag. She turned and shut the door without saying anything else. Gammon and Milton walked down the car.
Gammon looked at Milton, 'Thoughts, Sergeant?'

'What a strange lady, Sir.'

'Don't turn round but she is watching us from the upstairs landing window. Something isn't ringing true here, Sergeant.'

Gammon dropped Milton at Bixton Police station and decided to go and see Carol Lestar. Carol knew everybody and would have more information on Miss Alison, he was sure. As he pulled up at Carol's neat semi detached house in Swinster she was just coming out of the front door. 'After a date, Johnny boy?' she shouted.

'I'm just off to the Spinning Jenny for some lunch. I will treat you, Carol, I want a chat and I think you can help me.'

Sad Man
Second in the series of the
John Gammon Peak District Crime Thrillers

'Sounds exciting, John!'

The Spinning Jenny was quite full for a lunchtime. 'What are you drinking, Carol?'

'Seeing that I am going to help you, I'll have double vodka and diet coke please.'

'Ok, did you get that, Kev?'

'Certainly did, John, what about yourself?'

'Just diet Pepsi for me please, I am still on duty. Have you got a table for two?'

'Of course, always fit you in, John, especially that you are on a date,' and Kev flicked his red dickie bow and chuckled.

'What do you fancy, Carol?'

'I'm going to have the Barnsley Chop with mustard mash and country vegetables.'

'I'll have the Greek salad with cracked red wine potatoes please, Kev.'

'Ok, it won't be long, you two.'

Within fifteen minutes the meal arrived. Carol had another two double vodkas and was in full flow. 'Do you know of a Miss Alison from Micklock Moor?'

Sad Man
Second in the series of the
John Gammon Peak District Crime Thrillers

'Yes, John, why?'

'I can't say, it's just a line of enquiry I am following. What do you know about her?'

'She must be in her late seventies, early eighties now, John. She was left a big house and a lot of money when her father died. Think she is called Meredith, she has never socialised but there were rumours in the sixties that she had a baby by her father's accountant but I think it was just gossip. Her father would have made her give the baby away and the scandal would have been tremendous for the family.'

'Is the accountant still alive?'

'Oh no, John, he was in his late fifties when all these rumours started - he will be long gone.'

'Carol, please don't breathe a word of this to anyone.'

'Ok, fill my glass up then, this Barnsley Chop is superb.' It was three o'clock when John dropped Carol off at her semi in Swinster. Gammon decided to call it a day and went to see his Mum.

He pulled into the driveway to be met by Gyp. The dog was very excited to see John. Roger Glazeback was stood by the milking parlour with a mug of tea and a big piece of Emily's speciality Victoria Sponge cake. 'How are you, Roger?'

'Good thanks, Mr Gammon.'

'See Mum is looking after you.'

'She is a diamond your mother.' John smiled and entered the farmhouse kitchen.

His Mum flung her arms around him. 'Whoa, you ok, Mum?'

'You must have known, John, just been looking at some family holiday pictures - look at this one of you, Adam and your Dad on the beach at Bridlington. Do you remember? We used to stop at William Burrow's caravan - he was an old mate of your Dad's, they did National Service together. It was the only holiday we could afford! The caravan was very tatty and the roof leaked in but we had some great times.'

'I remember, Mum, William was a really nice guy - he wasn't married, was he?'

'No, he lived on his parents' farm and he had the caravan left him by his uncle so he never minded us going to stay. I know I should stop upsetting myself, John, but it is very hard, I miss your Dad and Adam so much, I am just thankful you decided to stay up here.'

Sad Man
Second in the series of the
John Gammon Peak District Crime Thrillers

'I know, Mum.' All the time his Mum was talking, he was thinking if the life he had back in London was what he really wanted but how could he leave his Mum now when she needed him so much?

'Anyway, enough of this silliness, do you want a cup of tea and a piece of cake, John?'

'Sure do, Mum, I saw Roger with a piece - it made my mouth water!'

'Sit down, then, let me sort you out. How is the job going? What a shame about that young girl, John.'

'Yes, very sad, Mum.'

'Are you any closer to catching whoever did this to these poor girls?'

'I have a few leads but nothing that could close the case, Mum.'

'I know you will get who did this, John, just hope it's soon before somebody else gets hurt.'

'Me too, Mum.' Emily gave John a very large slice of Victoria Sponge cake. It brought memories flooding back to the days when they were little and Philip and Emily would take them for a picnic. They would go to the beautiful Hittington-in-the-Dale stream. The boys would fish; Philip would have a bottle of beer and watch the boys while Emily set the picnic. He never thought that one day it would be just him and his Mum, or that Philip wasn't his blood father.

John polished off his cake and tea and made his way back. He decided that it might be a good idea to see if Joni was working so he headed for the Wobbly Man. John walked in to the Wobbly man and was met by Rick the landlord. 'Oh, John, poor Joni.'

'What's the problem?'

'Have you not heard?' She lost control of her car - apparently her brakes failed and she is in Derby Royal Hospital.'

'I didn't know, Rick, when did this happen?'

'About two hours ago.'

'Thanks, Rick, I better go and see what's happening.' John jumped in his car and called Carl Milton. 'Carl, have you heard about Joni?'

'Yes, Sir, I tried to call you but it kept going to answer phone.'

'I was at my mother's farm and they have very little signal. Apparently, I have just been told her brakes had been cut. Right, I want Brian Lund brought in for questioning, Milton, now.'

Sad Man
Second in the series of the
John Gammon Peak District Crime Thrillers

'Ok, Sir.'

'Leave him sweating with his lawyer while I nip and get an update on Joni at the hospital.'

'Will do, Sir.'

John rung off and as he did so his phone rang - it was Dave Smarty. 'Sir, I think you should know this, we were in the Drovers in Derby and Lund came in and I overheard him saying something like 'the stupid bitch has probably learnt her lesson, nobody plays with Brian Lund', I don't know if it means anything, Sir.'

'I have just had him arrested. The girl who stood up to him in the Wobbly Man last Sunday is in hospital - she lost control of her car and apparently her brakes were cut.'

'Ok, Sir, we will see you at the station.'

'I will be about an hour, leave him sweating, Smarty, then I want you in on the interview.'

'Ok, Sir, see you in a while.'

John asked at reception and found out that Joni was in Stanton Ward, bed number three. He made his way up the stairs to Stanton Ward - he could see Joni and she looked surprisingly good to say she was in a car accident. 'John, what are you doing here?'

'Two things; I wanted to see that you were ok, are you?'

'Twisted my ankle and I am a bit bruised but other than that I am ok. I had only just left home, luckily, and I braked for a cat and there was nothing there so I swerved to miss the cat and hit the wall.'

'It wasn't your fault, Joni, your brake pipes had been cut.'

'What!'

'I think I know who did it but not sure we will get a conviction.'

'Was it that Lund guy that I threw out of the Wobbly Man?'

'I think so but I have to prove it. Listen, if you are ok, I have arranged to have this guy picked up for questioning and they're waiting on me.'

'No problem, thanks for coming, we still on for Thursday?'

'Ok with me as long as you feel ok.'

'I will be fine, John.'

Sad Man
Second in the series of the
John Gammon Peak District Crime Thrillers

'Ok, I will pick you up at 8pm, we are booked in at the Spinning Jenny.'

John was seething inside as he raced back to Bixton Police Station, *this is another person close to me that this guy has hurt.* He arrived at the station and Desk Sergeant Hanney said Lund and his solicitor Mr Locke were in interview room one with Dave Smarty. Gammon entered the room and Dave Smarty reeled off the usual things to the tape and then said the time and date.

'Well, if it's not my old mate, Gammon, hope you are tending to the grave of that stupid brother of yours?'

'Mr Lund, I am not here to talk about my family, I am here to discuss your whereabouts last night and to maybe charge you with attempted murder.' Lund stood up and laughed in Gammons face. He had his big sweaty body close up and Gammon could smell the alcohol and stale cigarettes on Lund's breath.

Dave Smarty jumped up, 'Sit down this minute.' Again, Lund laughed but he did sit down. Mr Locke stated that he thought Mr Lund was being harassed by Bixton Police and he wanted this recording. Gammon had all on not blowing his lid at Locke for his defence of Lund but he stayed calm and carried on with the questioning.

Sad Man
Second in the series of the
John Gammon Peak District Crime Thrillers

Again he asked Lund of his whereabouts last night. This time Lund asked Gammon if he also looked after the prostitute's grave that Adam had been seeing. 'Mr Lund, you may not be aware, but the allegations you are facing are that you wilfully cut brake pipes of a car outside Surprise Cottage in Toad Holes with the intention of murdering one Joni Horalek who had an altercation with you in the Wobbly Man public house in Toad holes on Sunday afternoon. Do you deny these charges?'

'Some young lady refused to serve me in the Wobbly Man but I never cut her brakes - I don't even know who she is. Is she your missus, Gammon?' and he laughed again.

Locke turned to his client and whispered in his ear. 'Mr Gammon, do Bixton Police have any evidence that my client was involved in this despicable case and if not I suggest you release my client forthwith or I will be reporting a claim against Bixton Police for harassment of my client.'

Gammon nodded to Smarty to turn the tape off. 'Your client is free to go.'

Lund smirked at Gammon and Smarty, 'Tough luck, boys.'

Gammon leaned forward and spoke softly to Lund out of earshot of Locke. 'I will get you for what you have done, you fat pig, Lund, that's a promise to my brother and my father.'

Lund again laughed and said, 'Happy grave sitting, Gammon.'

Gammon came out of the interview room feeling quite down that yet again Lund was going to walk free when Sergeant Hanney called him over. 'Sir, we have a young lady and her mother in interview room three with Sergeant Di Trimble. The young girl says she has been raped.'

'Not again, Sergeant, ok, grab Inspector Scooper and tell her to come to the interview room.'

When Scooper and Gammon entered the interview room the girl's mother turned round and Gammon thought he knew her. For the tape, Scooper went through the procedure. 'So what is your name?'

'Lara Bennett.'

'And you are Jane Bennett?'

'I went to school with you, John. I was Jane Smythe.'

'I thought I recognised your face, Jane, sorry to meet in such unfortunate circumstances.'

Sad Man
Second in the series of the
John Gammon Peak District Crime Thrillers

'Thank you, John.'

'Right, what we need to do here, Lara, is ask you some questions then we have the doctor take a look at you if that's ok?' Lara nodded. 'Can I ask you what happened, Lara?'

'I was walking my dog on Micklock Moor about 7pm last night.'

'It's a bit late to be on your own up there, Lara,' Jane Bennett interrupted. 'I dropped her there - we have some horses on the moor so I went to feed them while Lara walked the dog.'

'So take your time, Lara, what happened?'

Holding back her tears, Lara explained that she had let her dog off the lead and as she bent down to pick up a stick for the dog somebody grabbed her from behind. 'I screamed but he put something over my mouth and nose and the next thing I knew...' Lara started crying.

'Just take your time, Lara, would you like a glass of water?'

'Yes, please.' Gammon signalled to Trimble to fetch a glass of water for Lara. Lara composed herself. 'When I came round, I could feel something heavy on my chest, my hands were tied and I had something in my mouth so that I couldn't shout. This thing in a black ski mask with red piping round the mouth hole was sat on me and he was laughing, I tried to struggle but I could see he had like barbed wire round his coat. After a short time he hit me because I was only half awake, I fell unconscious again and when I came round I was in a ploughed field and he had gone.'

'Could you take us to the field, Lara?'

'Yes, I know it quite well, it is next door to that big old house on the moor where Miss Alison lives - I know it because she owns lots of land round there but she wouldn't let me keep my horse on there when I asked her. If you look at the house it's the field on the left of the house about five fields away from where he drugged me.'

'Well done, Lara, we can save you the trauma of going back there now. I would like you to see the doctor now for a full examination.'

'Ok, can my Mum come with me, Mr Gammon?'

'Of course, Lara, thank you for being so brave.' John leaned toward Jane Bennett, 'I will be in touch, Jane.' Lara and Jane went down to the examination room. Gammon instructed Scooper to get a team to comb all the fields surrounding Miss Alison's house.

Sad Man
Second in the series of the
John Gammon Peak District Crime Thrillers

Gammon was starting to have suspicions about Miss Alison, *were the rumours true had she had a baby all those years ago and in that case did she live alone?* Maybe he should revisit again but first the gardener was to be questioned again.

'Evans, you and Trimble go and bring in the gardener from Miss Alison's house - he lives at the Old Poor House in Swinster and his name is Eric Stein.'

'Ok, Sir.'

Gammon then went to speak with Sergeant Hanney on the front desk. 'Pull up any records we have of a guy called Eric Stein please, Sergeant, he lives at the poor house in Swinster.'

'Eric Stein, now there is a blast from the past.'

'Why, do you know him?'

'Yes, I arrested him on a burglary and a rape charge back in the early eighties.'

'Was he done for it?'

'No, he actually got away on a technicality, Sir.'

'Explain, Sergeant, please.'

Sad Man
Second in the series of the
John Gammon Peak District Crime Thrillers

'Well it was before DNA was used and I had him bang to rights. He had broken into a house that he had done gardening and odd jobs at. He left a footprint which matched his trainer near the window where he broke in and there was also a fingerprint on the window.'

'Then what, Sergeant?'

'Well, we never found any other evidence other than the girl who was raped said she thought she knew her attacker. We did a line up and she picked Stein out. In court, his lawyer said that could not be admissible evidence because he worked at the house and the girl would have seen him about the premises.'

'What about the trainer print in the soil and finger print on the window?'

'Because we found no other evidence in the house, again the judge said Stein could have left a trainer print anywhere and could have touched the window while weeding the borders. I know it was him, Sir, but we just could not prove it.'

'Ok, let's look at his record. I see two stints in Leicester Prison for burglary. He also has one reprimand by a Sergeant Cully of this station for unruly behaviour but he was only cautioned. All these case go back thirty years and it appears he has been clean since. Ok, Sergeant, Stein is coming in for a chat. Give me a shout when he arrives and put him in interview room one.'

'Will do, Sir.'

Gammon climbed the stairs with the intention of seeing Max Allen to get him up to speed when a rough Scottish voice boomed out. 'Avoiding me, Gammon?'

'Just on my way to see you, Sir.'

'About bloody time, what is happening on the rape and murder cases?' Allen was an obnoxious man and John Gammon knew that Allen didn't like him but he tried to be professional. After Gammon had gone through the cases and where they were, Allen dropped his bombshell.

'Being my number two at the moment, you should know that I have taken a post in the North East, Gammon.'

'Really, Sir, why?'

'I have an elderly mother and it's a strain for me and the wife to be going backwards and forwards so I decided to apply for a vacancy in the North East near Sunderland which is only twenty minutes from my mother's home.'

Sad Man
Second in the series of the
John Gammon Peak District Crime Thrillers

'Sorry to see you go, Sir.' Gammon felt a bit like a fraud - he was actually over the moon. 'Who is coming here?'

'I haven't been told yet, Gammon, but I will put a word in for you.'

'Thank you, Sir.'

'How is Dave Smarty doing?'

'Seems a capable officer, Sir.'

'He will be a big asset for you, Gammon, trust me on this one.'

There was a knock on Allen's door - it was Sergeant Hanney, 'Your suspect is here, Sir, I have put him in Interview room one.'

'Thank you, Sergeant. I leave tomorrow, Gammon,' and at that, Allen stood up and shook Gammon's hand.

'So soon, Sir?'

'Yes but good luck, make sure you catch the evil son of a bitch.'

'Thanks, Sir, I will do my best.'

Gammon left the office and made his way down the corridor to the interview room where Inspector

Sad Man
Second in the series of the
John Gammon Peak District Crime Thrillers

Evans sat at one side of the table. Gammon joined him and Stein was at the other side. 'Mr Stein, I can make this informal or I can record it in which case you can have the choice of a lawyer or not.'

'Just get on with it. I know what this is about, I was a bloody stupid kid, it's a long time ago - don't you people ever give up?'

'Well, it's like this, Eric, we have had some young ladies raped we have had a murder and the girl was raped. So where were you on the nights in question? Because you work at Miss Alison's house gardening and all the rapes and the murder have taken place in a quarter of a mile of the house. You have previous form for alleged rape albeit no convictions for rape. Now tell me, Eric, where were you on these nights?' Inspector Evans recited the dates in question.

'Look, I live on my own, so I can't be sure but guessing I would have been watching the telly with a can of beer.'

'Can anyone vouch for you?'

'I just bloody told you, I live on my own.'

'So you won't mind if we search your house then, Eric?'

'Do what you like, I haven't done anything.'

Sad Man
Second in the series of the
John Gammon Peak District Crime Thrillers

'Inspector Evans, get Vaughan to search Mr Stein's property.'

'I want to be there, I don't bloody trust you lot, you will plant something in the house.'

'Ok, Eric, we will all go and you can watch the search.'

Gammon, Evans and Vaughan with Stein went to the Poor House in Swinster. 'We don't need the flashing blue lights, Inspector Evans.'

'Ok, Sir.' The Poor House had been a house where the poor people of the village would live if they could not support themselves; it was also known as the workhouse.

On arrival, Stein opened his front door. It was clear that he was a man living on his own; the living room had a big screen TV, a very old settee and a chair; the carpets were threadbare and on the coffee table there were plates with half eaten Chinese and pizza food on them. The kitchen sink was full of dirty pots and there was a table in the kitchen with clothes that appeared to have been washed but were drying. The house smelt of damp.

'Right, let's start in the kitchen. Eric, please feel free to watch.' The officers got to work and Evans quickly found a large knife under the sink.

Sad Man
Second in the series of the
John Gammon Peak District Crime Thrillers

'Is this a Bowie knife, Sir?'

'Yes, why?'

'Do you realise that this is illegal and is considered a dangerous weapon?'

'I use it in my job as a gardener.'

'Not anymore you don't,' Evans put the knife in a sample bag.

'Get it tested for DNA of any of the victims please, Inspector Evans.'

'Will do, Sir.'

They moved their way through the house but didn't find anything of consequence. 'Do you have any outside buildings, Eric?'

'Yes, two.'

'Can you open them, please?'

The first had been an old pigsty and the troughs were still in place. There was very little in this place, just a wheelbarrow and a strimmer.

'Open the other one, Eric.'

'I don't use that one, why do you need to go in there?'

Sad Man
Second in the series of the
John Gammon Peak District Crime Thrillers

'Either open it or I'll get a warrant to open it.' Finally Stein opened the shed. To everyone's amazement there was a large pin board with newspaper cuttings of the rapes and murders. 'So what have we here, Eric?'

'Look, I know how this looks – bad, but some years ago I was accused of rape and burglary and I wasn't guilty so I was let off and since then I have taken a morbid interest in any local case because honestly, Mr Gammon, I wasn't guilty last time but the guy who was, is probably the guy doing these things now.'

'Well that all seems convenient, Eric, trust me, we will be watching your every move. Ok, call the search off.' Gammon spoke with Inspector Evans as they walked down Stein's path. 'I want you to watch this guy for a few weeks, Paul. Make a dossier on his movements.'

'Ok, Sir, I am on the case.'

John called it a day and headed off to the Wobbly Man. John parked his beautiful Jaguar in the Wobbly Man car park and headed to the front door of the pub. As John entered the pub, he was met by Christos Minolis, the taxi driver, who appeared to be completely drunk. He bumped into Gammon then he pointed his finger directly at him in a slurred voice and said, 'It's because of you that I have no marriage now.'

'Mr Minolis, any problems in your marriage, you have created yourself, now please don't even consider driving that,' pointing at the taxi. 'Or even sit in it or I will arrest you, now - get out of my sight.' Minolis staggered out of the Wobbly Man and sat on one of the picnic tables with his head resting on his hands and he duly fell asleep.

John walked in to the bar to see that there were few early doors drinkers and Joni looking radiant. 'Hey, John, how are you?'

'Good thanks, Joni, I am just checking you are ok for the meal tomorrow night.'

'Yes, looking forward to it.'

'Ok, will pick you up at 7.30pm.'

'What are you drinking, John?'

'Nothing tonight, I need to call in at the Tow'd Man on my way home, its Denis's birthday and I'd like to buy him a beer.'

'Ok, I will see you tomorrow.'

'Look forward to it, Joni.'

Sad Man
Second in the series of the
John Gammon Peak District Crime Thrillers

John walked out and Cristos Minolis was still sat at the picnic table. He drove over the moors; it was a beautiful evening, *there is nowhere better than this when it is such a beautiful evening.* The Tow'd Man stood out on the moor - it had an early evening trade during the week, generally farmers after milking, a few quarrymen and a few truck drivers from Witters the local haulage firm.

John walked in the low beamed bar and was met by Denis. 'Hey, John, how are you?'

'Yeah I'm good, Denis.'

'You will like what I have on today - it's called Battery Blast from a local brewery.'

'Well actually, Denis, I have come to buy you a pint for your birthday.'

'Tha never forgets my birthday do you, lad, thanks very much - I will have a pint with you, I'm not working tonight.'

'So what are you having?'

'I'll have the Battery Blast - it's a session beer at 4.2%,' and he chuckled at the thought of a session at his age.

Sad Man
Second in the series of the
John Gammon Peak District Crime Thrillers

John brought the beers over and sat with Denis. 'Do you remember when you and young Lineman used to sell logs around the villages, John?'

'Flippin' heck, Denis, forgot about that.'

'You were a bloody pair in them days - totally inseparable.'

'Yeah, Steve has been a good mate.'

'Looks like he has dropped on his feet with his latest woman, John.'

'Yeah think so, Denis, and she is a nice girl as well - jammy buggar,' and they both laughed.

'Hutch up, you pair.'

'Ok, Clara, it's my birthday, you know!' The door creaked open and in came Steve and Jo followed by Carol Lestar, Cheryl and Lairy Bob.

John stood up, 'What are you all having?'

'I'll get these, John, must get Denis the Menace a beer or a top shelf.'

'You cheeky buggar, Stevie boy.'

'You wouldn't have me any other way, Denis. What are you having?'

Sad Man
Second in the series of the
John Gammon Peak District Crime Thrillers

'I better have a Bells whisky please, Steve.'

'Clara?'

'Same for me please, Steve.'

'John?'

'I'll have another pint of this Battery Blast.'

'Think I'll have one of them. What about you two Bob?'

'I'll try a Battery Blast. Cheryl?'

'Bacardi and Coke please, Steve.'

'Come on then, Lestar, what are you having?'

'Double Vodka and diet coke of course.'

'Silly me,' and Steve laughed. 'Jo?'

'Malibu and coke please.' Steve passed the drinks over and they raised their glasses to Denis and sang Happy Birthday.

Bob started his Pants on Your Head Routine, 'This is really good Denis.'

'Oh bloody hell, here we go. Go on then.'

'I got up this morning, went downstairs and dropped some ice cubes on the floor. Cheryl said 'what

Sad Man
Second in the series of the
John Gammon Peak District Crime Thrillers

have you done?' I said, don't worry it's just water under the fridge.' Bob laughed and they all chuckled.

'That's it now, Bob, we have heard them all before.'

'Don't be a spoil sport, Cheryl, my lovely.'

Just then, John's phone rang. 'Excuse me, I have to take this.'

It was Inspector Evans. 'Sorry to bother you, Sir, but there has been an arrest in Micklock. A guy got into a fight in the Queens Head and two constables arrested him - it is only Jimmy Reynolds, Sir.'

'Great, Evans, hold him on the affray ticket until tomorrow and I will interview him then. Great result, thanks - made my night.' John went back to the party and he must have looked pleased with himself.

'Hey, Porky, what's made your day?'

'Oh I may just have a breakthrough in the murder case.'

Before long, Denis was the worse for wear so Bob helped him to bed with Clara following and giving poor Denis untold grief about how bloody silly he was at his age. Jo offered John a lift, she had only had one drink so she said she would take everyone home.

They got outside and Jo proceeded to a brand new Range Rover Vogue, 'Hop in, you lot.'

'Blimey, Jo, this is some car.'

'Thanks, Cheryl, all my money came through from my aunty and I am pretty much set for life now.'

'You lucky girl, I am pleased for you, Jo.'

'Thanks, Carol.'

'Can you drop me in Swinster first please, Jo?'

'No problem, Carol, its better that way round anyway.' John was finally dropped off at 1.20am. He entered the cottage kitchen and poured a whisky - he didn't really need it but it had become a bit of a habit. He put it down to his loneliness at the cottage. In his mind it was as good an excuse as any.

The cottage was in good repair but the heating system wasn't the best so quite often John felt cold. It was something he had to tell the landlord but he had rented it through the estate agents Lowe and Harrison in Micklock and they said they always had problems getting in touch with the landlord in Derby.

Sad Man
Second in the series of the
John Gammon Peak District Crime Thrillers

John climbed into his comfy bed and settled down for the night. It was 4.45am when he was woken by the mobile ringing - his ring tone was Hey There Delilah by the Pretty T's a punk group. It had always reminded John of Lindsay - it would have been better that he changed it but he never got round to it. John switched on the bedside light and reached out for his phone. 'Hello Sir, it's Inspector Scooper, I am at work - it appears that the maniac has struck again.'

'Ok, Scooper, I am on my way.' He was just about to end the call when he realised he had no vehicle. 'Can you pick me up, Scooper?'

'Yes, Sir, no problem.' Scooper arrived in a small Renault Twingo. John climbed into the front seat but being a big guy he was pretty squashed. 'You ok, Sir?'

'Just drive, Scooper, and fill me in with the details.

'We were called out by a Mrs Denham, she said her daughter Mary had been attacked three nights ago by a man and she was badly cut but had managed to escape and hide in the wood until she thought he had left.'

'So where is she now?'

'They are at Bixton Police Station, Sir.'

Sad Man
Second in the series of the
John Gammon Peak District Crime Thrillers

Gammon was not feeling in the best of health after a night celebrating at the Tow'd Man and now he had Jim Reynolds to interview and a young girl Mary Denham. 'Scooper, call in Sergeant Milton and Sergeant Bannon. You and Bannon take Mary Denham's statement and I will deal with Jim Reynolds. Also, get Reynolds' lawyer over here seeing that we are all out of bed early.'

'Will do, Sir.'

'Ok, I will be in my office, shout me when we have everyone in the interview rooms.'

Feeling quite poorly, Gammon climbed the stairs to his office. He made himself a strong black coffee; he could feel his head pounding like there was a rugby match going on in his head. He slipped two Ibuprofen in to his mouth and swallowed them down with the black coffee. It was 5.40am when Scooper told Gammon they were set to go. Reynolds was in interview room two with Sergeant Milton. Gammon entered the room. 'For the tape, Superintendent Gammon has entered the room, time 5.43 am.'

'Well hello again, Jim, have you been on your holidays?'

'No comment.'

'Looking a bit dishevelled, Jim.'

Sad Man
Second in the series of the
John Gammon Peak District Crime Thrillers

Reynolds just looked at Gammon, his eyes were bulging and he looked possessed.

'Why has my client been brought in? I believe there have been no charges brought against him by the man who he had the altercation with.'

'All will be revealed in good time, Mr Cook.' Paul Cook was well know to the Bixton police - he was small in stature, approximately five foot eight with silver rimmed glasses and grey hair. He was well dressed and had made good money defending most of the scumbags from the local area. I would like an answer, Mr Gammon.'

'We would all like answers to what our Mr Reynolds has been up to, Mr Cook.'

'Ok, Jim, first things first, why did you leave the area when you were told you were a suspect in a murder and rape case?'

Cook leaned forward putting his hand to his mouth and spoke in Reynolds ear. 'No comment.'

'Getting a little tedious, Jim. Let me ask you, do you like abusing women - is that what you get off on?'

'No comment.'

'You see, Jim, we went to see your girlfriend when we were looking for you and she had been beaten quite badly and guess who she said had done this to her? You getting my line of thought here, Jim? You are a violent man and I think you like beating women and being in control.'

'No comment.'

'Really, Jim, no comment?' Reynolds then lost his temper, stood up and lifted the interview table of its legs scattering all the paper work. Sergeant Milton dropped Jim Reynolds to the ground and cuffed him. Cook stood shocked at his client's actions.

'Sit him up on the chair, Sergeant. You pull another stunt like that, Reynolds, and I will throw away the key, are we clear?' Jim Reynolds nodded. 'Shall we start again and let's cut the no comment bullshit shall we. What happened to Mrs Braint, your girlfriend?'

'She was going on about me going out too much and coming in late and I admit I have a temper. She was poking the fire and I don't know why, I grabbed her hand and as we swung round I caught her in the face with the poker. I just left and I then realised you lot would put two and two together and think I was this rapist guy because of my temper.'

Sad Man
Second in the series of the
John Gammon Peak District Crime Thrillers

'Well let me tell you something, Jim, Mrs Braint told us a slightly different story but she never reported you - it was noticed because we called at the house looking for you. So where have you been?'

'I have been sleeping rough.'

'And what happened last night in the bar?'

'My client does not need to answer that, Superintendent Gammon, there are no charges against him.'

'This guy was talking about Dana, Claire's daughter, that was raped - he said she was a minx and he knew her at school. I just lost it and two guys pulled me off him.'

'Well, I think we have heard enough now Jim. Where can we contact you?'

'Claire has said I can go back and Mr Gregory has let me go back to work at Witters.'

'You are a lucky man, Jim, but if you do a runner again I won't be so lenient. Interview ended.'

Gammon left the room and put his head round the interview room where Mary Denham was being interviewed by Inspector Scooper. 'A word please, inspector.' Scooper came out. 'How is it going?'

Sad Man
Second in the series of the
John Gammon Peak District Crime Thrillers

'Not too good, Sir, the mother seems very overpowering and the young girl is getting very upset.'

'What about Jim Reynolds, Sir?'

'I'm not a hundred per cent sure about this guy - we will have a team meeting after we have finished with Mary Denham - I'll come in with you.'

'Mary and Mrs Denham, this is Superintendent Gammon.'

'Pleased to meet you, Mr Gammon, you are quite famous in these parts.'

'Do you mind if I speak with Mary please, Mrs Denham? I want Mary to go through this with no interruptions please.' Scooper looked up to Gammon; he was so good at his job and deep down she had feelings for him that she dare not show.

'Well if it's like that, Mr Gammon, but as I was saying to your inspector...'

Gammon cut her short, 'As I said, Mrs Denham, I just want Mary's version please.' Mrs Denham sat back on her chair with a face like thunder. She closed her arms and just stared at Gammon.

Sad Man
Second in the series of the
John Gammon Peak District Crime Thrillers

'Now, Mary, take your time, and in your own words what happened three nights ago?'

'I was walking back from my friend's house in Micklock to the bus station - we live at Dilley Dale and 9.30pm is the last bus back home.' Mary then started to cry, her face was badly cut and she had a black eye although this had started to go down. Her hands and arms and legs were badly cut as if with a razor blade.

'Take your time, Mary.' Mary took a sip of water and carried on with the interview.

'I was a couple of minutes away from the bus depot and I always cut across the park by the bowling green and by the putting green where you pay the man for a game this man grabbed me and put something over my mouth, I remembered feeling drowsy.'

Mary got upset again and she took a few moments to compose herself. Swallowing hard she carried on with the interview. 'I found myself lay on some muddy grass with this thing on top of me and it was laughing, I am pretty sure it was a man.'

'How was he dressed, Mary?'

'He had a coat on like a raincoat, I tried to get him off me but there was something sewn in the coat that cut me when I tried. He had a ski mask on so I could not see his face. I remembered somebody telling me once that your eyes are the most vulnerable part of your body so I poked him as hard as I could in both eyes - he screamed and said something like 'bitch, I will kill you'. I knew I had one chance to get away so I ran into the woods. I realised where I was because I used to be a girl guide and we used to come for days to stay at the hut. I just ran and ran he wasn't particularly fast so I managed to get away. I hid in the bracken but he never came. I must have been there about two hours and I didn't see him or hear him so I used my mobile to phone Mum to come and get me.'

Gammon then brought Mrs Dunham in.

'Mrs Dunham, why didn't you call the police straight away?'

'I am chair of the Women's Institute and I am on the local parks and recreation committee and when the other girls were attacked people were saying it was their own fault, that they were tarty in skimpy clothes and I didn't want people saying that about my daughter.'

'I would just like to say, Mrs Dunham, that was very misguided - if we are to catch this maniac we needed to be at the scene of the crime straight away not three days later.'

Sad Man
Second in the series of the
John Gammon Peak District Crime Thrillers

'I am sorry, Mr Gammon.'

'Ok. Inspector, get the doctor to examine Mary and get these cuts sorted out for her. Come on, Mary, it's nearly over for you now. Interview ended. Thank you, Mrs Dunham, we will be in touch as and when we have any new information.'

It was now 9.10am and Gammon was just starting to come round. He headed for the coffee machine and as he walked past the Chief Constable's office, a familiar voice called him in.

'Vicky? What are you doing here?'

'They have sent me to replace Max Allen - they felt with my knowledge of the area and the current situation with this nutcase roaming the dales it would be a good idea.'

'Is it permanent?'

'They haven't said, why, would that be a problem?'

'No, of course not.'

'Well I think that is in the past, we have to be professional about this. Are you seeing anybody John?'

'Nothing serious. You?'

Sad Man
Second in the series of the
John Gammon Peak District Crime Thrillers

'Yes he is sales guy for a petrochemical company so travels the world a lot. We don't see loads of each other with his job and my job but that's ok. Pleased we can be straight with this, John.'

'No problem, ma'am.'

'Like that, John,' and she laughed. 'Right, update on this case please. Perhaps it would be better to have our meeting with everyone and we can go through everything. Just grab a coffee I'll meet you in the incident room.'

John stood in front of his team and when Vicky walked in nobody, he thought, knew much about their affair so it should be plain sailing. 'Ok, listen up everybody, Chief Constable Wills is back to help out since CC Allen has now left to take up his new post. So let's go through what we have please.'

'First victim Dana Braint, second victim Milan Peterson, both these girls were raped no DNA found, third victim Suzy Warner - raped and murdered. Fourth victim Lara Bennett, latest victim Mary Dunham, lucky for this young girl she fought her attacker off and other than cuts and bruises she will be ok. We haven't had the doctor's report but it's looking that way.'

'Suspects: Cristos Minolis, taxi driver, bit of a ladies' man; Jim Reynolds, lived with the first victim Dana's

Sad Man
Second in the series of the
John Gammon Peak District Crime Thrillers

mother, Claire Braint, violent man and possibly the main suspect; Eric Stein, local gardener - he has form for rape although not convicted still contests he never did it we have found a shed where he has newspaper cuttings of all rapes since he was convicted. This guy is a bit of a loner my hunch would be he has nothing to do with it but you never know so let's keep our minds open. Mark Anthony Tink, well-to-do parents, obviously spoilt boyfriend of Suzy Warner. Personally think he supplies drugs, we found drugs at his house which he said were Suzy's - we had him drug tested and he isn't a user so I took the decision to release him because I feel if we keep a close eye on this guy he will lead us to a bigger fish. Anybody like to add anything? Yes, Inspector Scooper?'

'Jim Reynolds - does his partner not want to press charges on the assault?'

'No, he is back living with her Inspector.'

'Well she is a fool then, Sir.'

'No accounting for taste, Scooper. If nobody has anything else to add I would like to discuss the Brian Lund situation if I may. Brian Lund as you are well aware I have personal issues with but I can assure the team it won't affect my professional judgement. Inspector Smarty has been watching

Sad Man
Second in the series of the
John Gammon Peak District Crime Thrillers

this scumbag for a couple of weeks now so I will let him fill everyone in on Lund.'

'First of all, can I just say welcome to the team, Ma'am.'

'Thank you, Inspector Smarty.'

'Well, I have watched Lund and his cronies now for a few weeks on and off. The guy is the lowest of the low - he is still running the girls on the streets in Derby. They arrive at different times of the evening and he takes them into a side room. Sometimes he comes out with the girl and he is laughing and sometimes he comes out and the girl will follow ten minutes later looking very upset. I am guessing if they have earned enough he is ok, if not I think he slaps them about. He has two guys with him that were arrested from the trouble in the Spinning Jenny the other Sunday - we now know them as Mickey Bloor, otherwise known as Mickey the knife for his use of said object. The other guy is called Robbie Stickler and this guy is a mean dude; he has previous for actual bodily harm and manslaughter - he served fifteen years in Durham for that one and got out about a year ago. He is a giant of a guy but our Superintendent managed to drop him with one blow on the day of the fracas in the Spinning Jenny.' The whole team applauded.

Sad Man
Second in the series of the
John Gammon Peak District Crime Thrillers

'I have seen drugs being sold and I did see a guy arrive with two heavies and a metal suitcase which when I looked him up he was a known drug dealer from Wales who goes by the name of Scotty Lomas. Lomas is well known but as yet nobody has ever made anything stick. Any case against him has been thrown out because any witness suddenly has memory loss or in the case of one witness he just disappeared.

'Just one other thing, I did see that guy on the incident board, Mark Anthony Tink, but I didn't see him talk to anyone - he just had a glass of red wine and then left. Lund wasn't there at the time he was. That's about all to report at the moment.'

'Ok, Inspector, good work, carry on with the surveillance. Let's just get out there see what we can dig up on the suspects.'

'Thanks, John, can we have a quick word?'

'Yes, Ma'am.'

'Just looking at the team, do you think there is enough experience in the squad?'

'Yes, I think so. As you know, Scooper and Evans had promotion; Smarty was brought up from Bristol by Max Allen; Bradbury, Cook, Trimble and Milton are all good officers, just quite new to Bixton.'

Sad Man
Second in the series of the
John Gammon Peak District Crime Thrillers

'I see we have Carl Milton at Bixton - I heard he single-handedly wiped out quite a nasty bunch of characters but his girlfriend died in the crossfire?'

'Yes, she did, Vicky, eventually they tried to save her but it didn't happen.'

'How has that affected him in his role as a police officer?'

'Personally, I think Carl will make a brilliant police officer - he has the guile and drive to succeed and I am more than impressed with him.'

'I take it you were less impressed with Max Allen - wasn't it because you felt you had been overlooked, John?'

'No, it really wasn't. Yes, I was annoyed at first but I got pass that. But the guy was an arse, he really was.'

'I have to tell you something in confidence, John.'

'What?'

'I pushed for you for this job when I left but the powers that be recognise you are an excellent detective but after the case that involved your brother Adam, there is a feeling that you covered certain things up to protect yourself and your family

Sad Man
Second in the series of the
John Gammon Peak District Crime Thrillers

so any promotion isn't going to happen in the future. I'm sorry, John.'

'Nothing surprises me anymore, Vicky, but thanks for the heads up.'

'Right, I have things to do.' Deep down John was fuming - not at Vicky but the stuffy establishment.

John left Vicky's office and was met by Sergeant Hanney. 'Sir, the doc left the results on the Dunham girl. There are no sign of any sexual activity, other than the cuts and bruises it appears she got away ok.'

'Well, that's good news, Sergeant.'

'Just one other thing, Sir.'

'Yes, Sergeant.'

'Would you sponsor me? I am doing the Swinster half marathon in aid of Swinster OAP's fund. They treat all the OAP's to a bus trip and a Christmas dinner every year.'

'I will not only sponsor you, Lee, but if you don't mind, I would like to take part.'

'That would be brilliant, Sir, you can register at the Spinning Jenny in Swinster - it's fifteen pounds to enter then just try and collect for a charity.'

Sad Man
Second in the series of the
John Gammon Peak District Crime Thrillers

'Great, when is the race?'

'It's this Saturday, Sir.'

'Blimey, that is short notice.'

'Have you run before, Sir?'

'Yes, quite a bit - I have done the London Marathon, the one in Gateshead and New York. I used to run for the Met.'

'Oh blimey, a professional, hey.'

'I just enjoy it, Lee.'

'I better get my skates on and sort it and some sponsorship. Thanks Sergeant, I will look forward to that. Right good night, Sergeant.'

'Good night, Sir.'

John climbed into his Jaguar and drove the scenic route back to his cottage. The route took him through Cowdale - it always reminded John of Adam, they used to play there with Steve Lineman. John was always a cowboy, Offside was always an Indian, and Adam had to be the sheriff. They played cowboys and Indians for hours in the old mill at Cowdale. *Happy days,* John thought.

As John drove down the winding roads to his cottage his mind wandered back to what Dave

Sad Man
Second in the series of the
John Gammon Peak District Crime Thrillers

Smarty had said about Mark Anthony Tink. *Why would he be in a back street boozer in Derby?* It wasn't near the shopping mall or anything and it is in a very rough area of Derby. John picked up his mobile and spoke with Inspector Evans, 'Paul, it's John Gammon, in the morning bring Mark Anthony Tink in for questioning, say 10am, I will be doing the interview.'

'Ok, Sir, what shall I say it's about?'

'Just tell him it is to help with our on-going investigations.'

'Ok, Sir, see you in the morning.'

John arrived at the cottage. Opening the front kitchen door he could see he had mail - most of it the usual rubbish; did he want a credit card, free coupons for a discount on washing powder at the Co-Op but amongst everything was a hand written letter. John opened the letter and inside was a note stating that it was from the Master.

Dear Mr Gammon, why are you and your plods so stupid? I am giving you the run around and you are no nearer to catching me than you were at day one. You, Johnny Boy, I watch you, I know everything about you but you know nothing about me.

Sad Man
Second in the series of the
John Gammon Peak District Crime Thrillers

I want you to tell the press that The
Master has contacted you so they know
what to call me on the news. If you
don't, I will kill again. You have
one week to sort it, Johnny Boy. ☺

John immediately called Vicky Wills and filled her in on the letter. She told John to sleep on it and that they would talk in the morning before releasing anything. John looked at the clock - it was now 7.05pm and he needed to shave, shower and pick Joni up for the meal. He rushed upstairs, quickly shaved and showered and was out of the house by 7.15pm. John had his Paul Smith dark blue suit on and a John Rocha light blue shirt he wore his favourite black Kurt Geiger shoes. He arrived at Joni's spot at 7.30pm to find her waiting by the gate. She looked incredible; she had a black dress with a short, cropped yellow cardigan and a pair of black stiletto heeled shoes.

Joni climbed in the Jaguar and gave John a peck on the cheek. 'I thought you weren't going to make it, John.'

'Sorry, Joni, work always gets in the way.'

'No problem, we are on our way now.'

They arrived at the Spinning Jenny and were met by Doreen. 'How are you two tonight? You both

Sad Man
Second in the series of the
John Gammon Peak District Crime Thrillers

look like movie stars. Do you want to come straight through to the dining room? I have put you in the corner overlooking Hittington Dale through the big picture window. We have the rugby club dinner in tonight so it may get a little rowdy - hope you don't mind.'

'No problem, Doreen.'

'Ok, I will give you a minute, would you like a drink?'

'Do you like wine, Joni?'

'Yes I like red wine, John.'

'Ok, Doreen, can we have a bottle of Rioja please?'

'Coming up.'

John did the gentlemanly thing and pulled the chair out to let Joni sit down. They opened the menus. After a few minutes Doreen was back and John got Joni to taste the wine - she was happy. 'Any thoughts on food yet, or do you want a minute?'

'I am ready, what about you, Joni?'

'Yes, I know what I am having.'

'Ok, fire away.'

Sad Man
Second in the series of the
John Gammon Peak District Crime Thrillers

'Can I have buffalo mozzarella, heritage tomato and pickled cucumber on a bed of crispy lettuce please?'

'And for you, John?'

'I will have vanilla oil poached hake fillet with asparagus tips please, Doreen.'

'Now mains please.'

'Can I have roast 'Aylesbury' duck breast, beetroot glaze, celeriac puree, tenderstem broccoli with Swinster creamed mash potato please?'

'You can, my dear, and for John?'

'I think I will stick with fish so can I have pan fried 'Cornish' lemon sole, confit fennel, baby beetroots and barrel shaped roast potatoes please.'

'Ok you two, sit and enjoy the view while we get you set up with your meal.'

'Thanks, Doreen.'

'I like the menu, John, they have changed it a bit.'

'Apparently the old chef who has been here fifteen years and basically built the restaurant up rotired last week so they have a new guy from Pritwich - Richie Jewelitt who worked under Michel Braze the top London chef in Knightsbridge at the famous White Cabbage restaurant.'

'How do you know all this?'

'I used to eat there once a month so I got to know Richie quite well and it turned out he had a house in Pritwich so we used to talk about Derbyshire a lot and apparently he decided he wanted to come over this way. Doreen and Kevin were looking for a chef so I let him know. He really is a top chef so Kev and Doreen are very lucky to have him.'

Doreen arrived with the starters. 'Oh, John, this is fabulous.'

'Told you he was good. So how did you get to know Beth, the novelist who lived in Rita Butts cottage?'

'She just came in the Wobbly Man one night with Carl Milton. I have known Carl for years, pretty much grew up together so we're good friends.'

'Yes, Carl seems a nice guy - it must have been a massive blow to him when Beth died.

'Yeah, that pretty much broke his heart, John. I hear you were married.'

'Yes, to Lindsay but we are divorced now.'

Sad Man
Second in the series of the
John Gammon Peak District Crime Thrillers

'Any children?'

'No, luckily.'

'What went wrong there? Oh I am sorry, John, I should not have asked that.'

'No problem, Joni, she went off with someone else - it's a long story, to be honest, my job means I work unsociable hours and I think Lindsay got bored of it.'

'Well it's her loss, John.'

'Nice of you to say that.'

'You two finished?'

'That was excellent, Doreen, thanks.'

'What about you, Joni?'

'Absolutely fabulous, Doreen.'

'Great, well, that's a good start. The rugby boys have just arrived so the noise level may go up. Back in a minute with your mains.'

'Thanks, Doreen.'

The rugby boys sat down - there were about twenty-four men and their wives and girlfriends.

Sad Man
Second in the series of the
John Gammon Peak District Crime Thrillers

'You have gone quiet.'

'Oh it's nothing really, when I was seventeen I was engaged to the big guy sat on the right hand side of the table.'

'The one with blonde hair and Ralph Lauren polo shirt?'

'No, John it's the dark haired guy - he has a sports jacket on with leather arm pads.'

'Oh I can see him, he seems quiet.'

'He isn't, John, and generally after we split, he would always cause trouble with any guy I was with.'

'Don't worry about it, Joni, I am a big boy.'

'I know, it just ends up ruining everyone's night.'

Doreen arrived with the mains, 'That's yours, John, the fish, and the duck breast for you, Joni. Right, enjoy, I better go and sort that lot out.' The evening went well; no trouble with Joni's ex and the meal was fabulous. Joni finished off with Raspberry Crème Brule on a shortbread biscuit and John had Pumpkin Roll with strawberries and pouring cream. They followed that with coffee and a small luxury Thornton's chocolate which John though was a nice touch.

Sad Man
Second in the series of the
John Gammon Peak District Crime Thrillers

John paid the bill and as they were leaving the chef came out to say goodnight to John. 'Thanks for coming, John, hope you both enjoyed your meals.'

'Richie, this is Joni.' Richie shook hands with Joni she thought he looked about forty-eight. He was a stocky guy with a nice smile. John later told Joni Richie was actually fifty-nine.

John drove Joni home. 'Do you fancy a night cap, John?'

'If you are offering.'

They opened the kitchen door at Surprise view and within seconds they were in an embrace. Things really hotted up and they made love on the pine kitchen table. Joni was full of apologies, 'That really is not like me, John, I have never done that on a first date, not even a fourth date, I don't think.'

'We are both adults, Joni, I am very flattered,' and he kissed her again.

'Are you going to stay the night?'

'If you want me too.' They opened another bottle of red and sat and talked.

'John, I have to tell somebody. I have been left an enormous amount of money by Beth Elliot - she was such a wonderful friend to me and now she has gone. Until you came along, I really didn't know what to do with myself - I had thought about going away but then poor Carl is so in bits I couldn't do that too him.'

John thought it best not to mention about Carl and the money. 'Beth would want you to have a lovely life, Joni, that's why she has done this for you.'

'I know, John, but what kindness.' Joni laid her head on John's shoulder and they were both soon asleep. It was 6am when John woke up and decided he better get back home and get changed; he had the interview with Tink at 10.00am. He thanked Joni for a nice evening and asked if she fancied going walking on Sunday morning, which she said she would. As she waved John off, she felt like she was in a dream - she had found the one man she thought could make her happy.

John got in his car but for some reason he felt sad. He didn't know why he had these feelings - he had a great night with Joni. He wasn't sure if talking about Lindsay had made him realise he was carrying a torch for her still or was it the fact that Vicky Wills had got over him so quickly - either way he should have been feeling happy, not sad. John drove home and changed for work.

Sad Man
Second in the series of the
John Gammon Peak District Crime Thrillers

Sergeant Hanney met him at the front desk, 'Mark Anthony Tink is in interview room one with his lawyer and his parents, Sir.'

'Oh great, thanks, Sergeant.'

Mrs Tink was the first to harangue Gammon. 'Why is my son being held here - is he a suspect? We told you everything. He ran away because he thought we would be mad about him crashing the Porsche.'

'I think that is the least of Mark's problems, Mrs Tink, now if you will excuse me, I have things to do.'

Gammon entered the interview room to see Tink looking nervous. 'Can you tell me why you are holding my client, Superintendent Gammon?' Gammon knew this was a top lawyer; he had come across him in London on a case.

'Well, Mr Tundy, the last time we spoke with Mark he told us that the cocaine found in his bedroom was actually Suzy Warner's but I now believe that to be untrue.'

'I wasn't lying, Mr Gammon.'

'How have you come to this conclusion, Superintendent?' Gammon ignored the solicitor and asked Tink if he had ever been in a pub in Derby called The Drovers Arms.

Sad Man
Second in the series of the
John Gammon Peak District Crime Thrillers

'No, I haven't, Mr Gammon.'

'Do you want me to ask that question again and give your some time to think?' Tink looked at Tundy who nodded as much as to say answer truthfully.

'Ok, I sometimes go in there for some personal weed. I used to call with my mates from Derby University. But that's all, Mr Gammon, and it's only for personal use.'

'Doesn't make it anymore legal, Mark.'

'I know and I am sorry I lied to you.'

'Do you know somebody called Brian Lund, Mark?'

'Yes, he is the guy who we buy weed off.'

'I would just like a moment to speak with my Chief Constable. Interview suspended, 11.20am.'

'Inspector Evans, sort some drinks out for Mr Tink and Mr Tundy please, I will only be a few moments.' Gammon raced up to Vicky Wills's office. 'Vicky, I think I have a chance of nailing Brian Lund for supplying a class A drug but I need your ok to do it.' Gammon explained that one of the suspects Tink bought weed off Brian Lund at the Drovers arms and if he could get him to wear a wire and ask Lund

Sad Man
Second in the series of the
John Gammon Peak District Crime Thrillers

for cocaine then they would have Lund nailed and could let Tink off on the marijuana charges.

'Go for it, John, that's fine by me - you deserve this chance.'

Gammon could feel his heart beating fast; he knew this was a great chance for him. Gammon re-entered the interview room. Evans did the tape and Gammon laid his cards on the table. 'This is the situation Mark, we have you on tape admitting that you buy drugs and we found cocaine in your bedroom, which I now believe was yours.'

'That's just not true, Mr Gammon.'

'Well, true or not, we have you bang to rights unless of course you want to cooperate with us.'

'What are you asking my client to do, Superintendent?'

'We want him to wear a wire and to record buying cocaine off Brian Lund.'

'And what does my client get in return?'

'All charges dropped with regard to possession and use of a Class A drug.'

Sad Man
Second in the series of the
John Gammon Peak District Crime Thrillers

Tink and Tundy quietly spoke to each other. 'My client is willing to do this only if his identity is not compromised at the trial.'

'Fine by me, Mr Tundy.'

'Ok, Mr Gammon, we have a deal.'

'When would you normally buy weed from Lund?'

'Thursday or Friday night.'

'Right, let's go for tonight with it being Friday - we will wire you and I will tell you what we want you to say.'

Gammon arranged for Tink to be wired and it was now 5.30pm. 'Go in your own car, Mr Tink and Sergeant Milton will come with you.'

Gammon could feel the elation inside him - at last he would nail the bastard that created this shitstorm for his family. Gammon told Wills the plan and she stated she wanted officers in the pub and armed response outside. Gammon spoke with Smarty and Scooper and arranged for them to act like a couple in the pub.

Smarty and Scooper were already in the pub holding hands to look like a couple, although they did stand out a bit, as this was a real rough pub. It was 8.15pm when Mark Anthony Tink came into the

Sad Man
Second in the series of the
John Gammon Peak District Crime Thrillers

pub. He sat at the bar and ordered a beer. After twenty minutes a big guy walked over to him and he got off his stool and disappeared in the back. Ten minutes passed and there was no sign of Tink. Dave Smarty walked up to the bar to see if he could see anything but the door was shut. Both Smarty and Scooper were not sure what to do so they decided to go and find Tink.

As they went towards the back room, they were met by the barman. 'Sorry, that's not open to the public.' Smarty flashed his warrant card and pushed the door open fully expecting trouble. 'Hey,' the barman shouted, 'What are you doing?'

The room was empty other than a television playing in the corner. 'Where has the big guy and the guy sat at the bar gone?'

'Sorry, mate, I don't know, I only work Friday and Saturday nights.'

'Who was the big guy?'

'I never noticed anyone. I served the young guy when he came in but I have been busy so I am sorry but I can't help you.'

Scooper got on the radio to Gammon. 'We have lost him, Sir, he disappeared with a big guy.'

'Shit, Scooper, how the hell did this happen?'

Sad Man
Second in the series of the
John Gammon Peak District Crime Thrillers

'Sorry, Sir, but he went in the back with a guy so we gave him ten minutes to come out and he didn't so by the time we went in they must have slipped out the back.'

'That little weasel, wait until I catch up with him, abort the operation.' Gammon was seething; he stood down the operation and now had to explain to Wills. He phoned Wills, 'Ma'am, it's Superintendent Gammon, I am afraid we lost Tink - he must have gone out the back way so until we can find him there's nothing more we can do. I have instructed Derby police and Bixton to put out a search for him but he has probably gone to ground with his drug friends.'

'Ok, John, well bad luck on that one - I know how much it means to you to get Lund but be patient, we will get him some day. Go and enjoy your weekend.'

'Thanks, Vicky, you too, see you Monday.' John spoke with Scooper and Smarty just to put the record straight that he wasn't blaming them for the debacle. It was now 9.35pm so John decided to call at the Tow'd Man on his way home. He wanted to call and spend some time with his Mum on Saturday.

John walked in the bar and was met by Denis. 'Now then, Denis, have you recovered?'

154

Sad Man
Second in the series of the
John Gammon Peak District Crime Thrillers

'Don't you bloody start, had enough stick off your mate in the other end with Bob.'

'Oh I better see if they want a drink.' John put his head round the corner to see that the usual crowd were in: Carol Lestar, Bob and Cheryl, Steve and Jo, and Jack and Shelley Etchings from Ardwalk. Straight away Shelley planted a kiss on John's cheek. They had been in the pub since 7pm according to Steve and they were all pretty much on their way.

'We have a mini bus booked for 12.30am, John, come home with us and Steve will pick you up in the morning to get your car.'

'Thanks, Jo, that sounds like a good idea. Right, what's everyone having?'

'Double Vodka and diet coke please, lover-boy.'

'Ha ha, very good, Carol. Jo?'

'I'm drinking White Zinfandel by Barefoot, John.'

'Do you need another bottle?'

'Go on then, thanks.'

'Shelley?'

'Brandy and port for me with a spot of lemonade.'

Sad Man
Second in the series of the
John Gammon Peak District Crime Thrillers

'Cheryl?'

'Can I have a Bacardi and coke please, John? Don't want to get wrecked like last time.'

'Oh the cutey pie time, Chez.'

'Knew you would bloody remember, Lineman,' and she laughed.

'Jack?'

'Pint of Pedigree, John please.'

'Bob?'

'Stella for me, John, thanks.'

'Steve?'

'I'm on Mucky Duck, it's well nice, John.'

'Ok, make that two of them please, Denis.'

By 10.15pm they were in full swing with Bob trying to tell one of his jokes and Cheryl telling him they didn't want to hear anymore. Steve and Jo were dancing to You To Me Are Everything by the Real Thing, and Jack, Shelley and Carol were sat with John. 'Come on then, John, who is the new love of your life? I saw Jeanette the other day she said if I saw you to say 'hi'.'

Sad Man
Second in the series of the
John Gammon Peak District Crime Thrillers

'I must pop down and see her, it's been ages and yes, we are still friends.'

'That's good then, John.'

'Yeah, Shelley, I guess we always will be there for one another.'

'Come on then, what about the barmaid from the Wobbly, then lover boy?'

'What do you want to know, Carol?'

'Well, is it serious? She is very pretty - didn't her Aunty used to be the head teacher at Pritwich primary school - what was her name, Shelley?'

'Miss Manly, think her first mane was Marcy - she always smelt nice when we were little - she always wore perfume do you remember?'

'Did she ever get married?'

'No, I don't think so, Shelley.'

'That's where Joni must get her looks from, Carol.'

'Definitely, her Aunty was stunning and such a lovely person. Only ever saw her get angry once and that woo with Kev from the Spinning Jenny - he would only have been about eight and he was firing elastic bands at the chalk board as she was writing

Sad Man
Second in the series of the
John Gammon Peak District Crime Thrillers

so she rolled up his short trousers and slapped his legs so hard it left a hand print.'

'You couldn't do that these days, Carol.'

'I know, but that's why we are in such a mess, Jack.' The whole table agreed on that.

'Have you got any Motown, Clara?'

'I'll get Denis to look - he is in charge of the music.'

'Chain Reaction by Diana Ross please, Denis.'

'Hold your horses, Carol, while I find my glasses.' Denis found the CD and the whole pub started dancing. By this time, poor Cheryl was again the worse for wear. Bob was wobbling as he danced so he was a bit oblivious to Cheryl stroking his cheek and calling him cutey pie but Carol Lestar picked up on it and asked Denis to make a request for Cutey Pie. Denis duly obliged which left everyone in hysterics.

It was 12.30am and Russell from Cowdale Coaches started rounding up everyone. Shelley and Jack, although a little worse for wear, got on the mini bus ok. Steve, Jo and John were next. Carol was holding up Cheryl with Bob who was also staggering. 'Good night, Denis.'

'Thanks everyone for coming.'

Sad Man
Second in the series of the
John Gammon Peak District Crime Thrillers

'See you soon, Den.'

'Ok, Steve, look after that pretty lady.'

'Oh I will, Den.'

John sat behind Steve and Jo. 'Are you about Sunday? Me and Joni are going walking and thought we might drop in for a coffee.'

'That would be great, John, Steve needs to nip to B&Q for some paint at around eleven, but we will be about.'

'We should be there about 1pm I am guessing, Jo.'

'Great, look forward to it.'

The mini bus dropped John off and pulled away up his drive. It was a beautiful full moon. John sat at the little table overlooking the valley. The valley had an eerie feel about it. The moon was casting shadows all over the Peaks and the stars were bright and twinkling like diamonds in a jewellers shop. John sat there for an hour then decided it was bedtime; he was just glad he hadn't started drinking at 7pm like the rest of the gang.

It was 10am on Saturday morning and John was still in a deep sleep when he heard a knocking at the door. He quickly put his bathrobe on and climbed downstairs - it was a guy from UPS. 'Parcel for a Mr John Gammon.'

'That's me.'

'Can you sign and print your name there please, Sir?'

'Thank you,' and John took the shoebox-size parcel into the kitchen. John opened the parcel and inside was a Barbie doll with her head cut off and tucked under her arm. John opened the note inside it just said 'I warned you, Gammon'.

John immediately called Vicky Wills. After explaining what he had received they arranged to meet at Bixton Police Station. John called Sergeant Milton in. 'I want a full DNA test on this parcel - we need something from this, Carl.'

'Ok, Sir, I will do my best.'

'What are your thoughts, Vicky?'

'To be honest, John, I am not convinced that this is our rapist or killer. Somebody is trying to play with your head.'

'To be fair, Vicky, they are not doing a bad job of that. Who else is it if it's not our killer?'

'It could be Jim Reynolds, Cristos Minolis or even the Tink boy.'

'Have they found Tink yet?'

'No, John, but his car was not left at the Drovers car park either - we have plenty of resources out looking for him and the pub is being watched. What about Lund - could he be doing this?'

'I really don't know, Vicky, the sooner I get that scumbag off the streets the better for everyone.'

'We will, John, just be patient.'

'I am just frustrated.'

'Well there is nothing we can do until we get the DNA results back on Monday so we may as well call it a day. We are certainly not pandering to this guy with regard to contacting the newspapers and giving him a name tag that's for sure.'

'Agree, Vicky.'

'Ok, well enjoy the rest of the weekend.'

'Will do, see you Monday.'

John left the station and headed for his Mum's farm. The drive over there was one of the most

Sad Man
Second in the series of the
John Gammon Peak District Crime Thrillers

scenic drives he thought anyone could make in the world but he still yearned for London and the bright lights. That wasn't an option until his Mum was sorted. He pulled into the farmyard and Gyp the collie dog walked over - he was getting old now and was not as lively as before but was still happy to see John.

'Hi John,' Emily came over to John wiping her hands on her pinafore. 'Are you staying for some lunch?'

'That was the plan, Mum.'

'Great, I have a lovely cottage pie.' Emily and John went in the kitchen. It was always special; the kitchen always smelt of homemade bread and Emily was a really good cook. John sat down and Emily came out with the biggest cottage pie that could feed a family of eight.

'Blimey, Mum, this is a big pie!'

'I know, John, I can't get used to not cooking for your Dad and Adam so I still make the same and give Roger Glazeback and his son some to take home.'

'You are soft, Mum.'

'I know, but Roger has been so good, I don't know what I would have done without him.'

Sad Man
Second in the series of the
John Gammon Peak District Crime Thrillers

'Mum, can I ask a question?'

'Yes, son, what is it?'

'Well, I have a couple of questions. What have you decided to do about the farm? And at Dads funeral, did Uncle Graham say anything to you about me?'

'I thought you had let that go, John.'

'I know, Mum, but he is an old guy now and maybe I should speak with him.'

'Your Uncle Graham is seventy-one, John, I said before - it's your decision, nobody can be hurt now.'

'I need to think on it, Mum. What about the farm?'

'Well, Roger has asked if he could rent it off me.'

'Can he afford it, Mum?'

'I don't think he can but if I go down that route I would certainly give him first refusal. I think you are right though, son, I should give myself more time.'

With the cottage pie demolished, John was given homemade Bakewell tart by his Mum with custard. 'You haven't lost your touch, Mum '

'Thanks, son, it's lovely to see you sat at the table enjoying a meal I have cooked.'

Sad Man
Second in the series of the
John Gammon Peak District Crime Thrillers

Just then John's mobile rang it was Joni. 'Hey, how are you?'

'Great thanks, John, sorry to bother you but I wondered if you fancied some lunch - I am working tonight at the Wobbly.'

'Oh, Joni, I'm sorry; I have just eaten at my Mum's. But tell you what; I will pop in for a quick drink tonight to see you.'

'Ok, John, see you tonight.' John could sense the disappointment in Joni's voice.

'I hear you have a new girlfriend.'

'Well, not really a girlfriend, Mum, we have only been out a couple of times.'

'Joni Horalek, isn't it?'

'How did you know?'

'Oh, the village jungle drums, John.'

'Who was it, Mum?'

'Do you remember Christine Benshaw? Well, her son was at the Spinning Jenny having a meal and he told his Mum he plays rugby so was at some party.'

'How would he know me?'

Sad Man
Second in the series of the
John Gammon Peak District Crime Thrillers

'After the last case and our Adam, I think everyone round her knows John Gammon, son. Your Grandad would have been proud of you.'

'Wasn't granddad a police man?'

'Well, military police, son.'

'Oh yes, I remember now. Well, Mum, I better get my skates on.'

'What are you on with today?'

'I need to put some washing in and I am going to nip and see Jeanette.'

'I liked Jeanette she has always been such a good girl to her parents.'

'Right, Mum,' and John gave his Mum a peck on the cheek and a hug. 'I will call you in the week.'

'Bye, son, be careful.'

John drove down the valley eventually arriving at Dilley Dale Ices. The courtyard was packed with walkers having light refreshments and ice creams. Jeanette was clearing a table and she spotted John. 'Hey, John, how are you?' Putting down her dishcloth, she walked over and gave John a peck on the cheek.

Sad Man
Second in the series of the
John Gammon Peak District Crime Thrillers

'Yeah, I'm pretty good thank you. It looks like business is good, Jeanette.'

'Yes, best thing we ever did, John. Do you fancy a coffee and a piece of homemade trifle cake? Well Cheryl and Jackie made it next door actually.'

'I will have a coffee but no cake - I am absolutely stuffed - been to lunch at Mum's.'

'Ok, come on in.' Jeanette brought a coffee for John and a tea for herself.

'How are things then, John? Are you still seeing Vicky...? Sorry not being funny, can't remember her surname.'

'Wills. No, we split quite some time ago.'

'Anyone else on the horizon?'

'I have been out for a drink with Joni Horalek a couple of times.'

'Doesn't she live in Toad Holes?'

'Yes at the top of the hill.'

'I know, behind that writer girl, Rita Butts place.'

'Yes, that's correct.'

'Bit young for you, Mr Gammon,' and she laughed.

Sad Man
Second in the series of the
John Gammon Peak District Crime Thrillers

'Joni is only three years younger.'

'Pretty girl, if I remember correctly. There was a silence after that sentence then Jeanette said, 'I am pleased we are still mates, I would have hated to have lost your friendship, John.'

'That will never happen, Jeanette.'

'Well if you ever fancy going for a walk, you know where I am, John.'

'I will bear that in mind, mate.' Their conversation lasted almost an hour until Jeanette had to carry on with it being so busy.

'Thanks for the drink.'

'Nice to see you, John, don't be a stranger.'

It was 7.15pm so John drove down to the Wobbly Man at Toad Holes to just double check that Joni was ok for their walk Sunday. John walked in and could see Cristos Minolis sat at the bar again looking worse for wear. Joni came over. 'Oh, John, so glad you have called in, I have been calling you.' John looked at his phone he had accidently switched his mobile to mute. There were eight missed calls from Joni.

'Sorry, I must have caught my phone and switched it off - what's the matter?'

Sad Man
Second in the series of the
John Gammon Peak District Crime Thrillers

'The guy at the bar - he has been saying since I came on shift that he is going to kill Gammon the copper. He says he has a gun, John.'

Luckily the bar was half empty with it being so early in the evening. 'Mr Minolis, I believe you want to speak to me?'

'Gammon, I hate you, I have lost everything because of you and you will pay I promise you this.'

'Well, Mr Minolis, I believe you have a gun, is that correct?'

'Yes, that's correct, copper, and I will blow you away one day.'

'Well, I am a serving police officer and I am arresting you for threatening behaviour towards a police officer and if we find you are armed then you will be dealt with accordingly.' Minolis tried to take a punch at Gammon but missed and fell flat on his face. John got on the phone to Bixton to send a car around to arrest Minolis.

The police arrived and took him away. John said to keep him forty-eight hours, which will take it to Monday and he will formally charge him then. 'Right, Joni, now I only called in to see if you are ok for the walk tomorrow.'

'Yes, looking forward to it, where are we going?'

Sad Man
Second in the series of the
John Gammon Peak District Crime Thrillers

'That's a surprise.'

'Man of mystery hey, John.'

'That's me,' and they both laughed. 'Be at my place for ten in the morning, Joni.'

'Great, will see you then.' John stayed about an hour then left for the Tow'd Man.

'Evening, Denis.'

'Hello, John, bloody music's too loud again.' Denis wasn't much of a loud music man.

'Who is playing Denis?'

'A couple of local lasses; Amy Lucy Amy and Lucy Amy Lucy.'

'That's their names, Denis?'

'That's their real name but they call themselves. The Wine-Drinking Leg Irons. They sound very good. They have nice voices but are too bloody loud for me.' John got himself a drink and popped his head round the corner to see the group line-up. There were two girls on guitars, a drummer and a keyboard player. They finished playing their song and the lead singer introduced the band.

'Ladies and Gentlemen, thanks for coming to support us tonight, I would like to introduce the

Sad Man
Second in the series of the
John Gammon Peak District Crime Thrillers

band members; on drums we have the famous Calum Treefit, and on keyboards Joanne Treefit. You may have guessed that they are son and mother. To my left, sharing vocals and bass guitar - my lovely twin sister Amy Lucy Amy and that just leaves me on lead guitar and vocals Lucy Amy Lucy. Ya'all ready for a great night? Let's kick this evening off with a Neil Diamond number, a big favourite in these parts "Sweet Caroline".'

The place was rocking - Lucy and Amy's voices were very powerful - the whole pub was dancing and singing. Carol Lestar came over. 'Hi, John, no Joni tonight?'

'She is working at the Wobbly, Carol.'

'So I have you all to myself, hey,' and she laughed.

'Guess so, mate.' John scanned the pub for a get out excuse. He noticed Carl Milton sat on his own in a corner so he wandered over. 'Do you mind if I sit with you, Carl?'

'No, Sir.'

'Please, it's John out of work. What are you doing so far away from Toad Holes?'

'Just having a beer, my Mum dropped me off and I've been a bit down today over Beth so I'm drowning my sorrows I guess.'

Sad Man
Second in the series of the
John Gammon Peak District Crime Thrillers

'Let me get you one.' John got up and as he did he felt something crack in his knee and had to sit down again. 'Blast, that hasn't happened in years.'

'What's the problem?'

'It's my left knee, it will be fine if I sit for a while, it's just breaks down on me every now and again. I did it playing squash years ago.'

'Let me get to the bar. Shall I put you one in, John?' John declined the offer. Carl stood next Tony Sheriff at the bar doing a bit of brown nosing round the gaffer.

'Hey Carlos.'

'It can't harm my promotion chances, Tony,' and he laughed.

Carl sat back down with John. 'So, Carl, have you decided what to do about Rita Butts's cottage?'

'I spoke with Rita and she said she would have it valued. She did say she didn't really want to sell it. Anyway, I went to watch Derby County this afternoon and when I got back there was a letter from Mrs Butts. She said the cottage had been valued at £440 950 - way above what I can afford, I only rent mine in the village. Anyway, the letter goes on to say how much she thought of Beth and what a lovely couple we were and that we reminded her of her and her husband. She said because of what had happened, I could have the cottage for £240,000. I don't know what to do, John, I feel I am ripping her off.'

'Well, I know, Carl, but at the end of the day I read into this that she wants you to have the cottage after all you have been through.'

'So you think I should go for it, John?'

'Actually, I do, Carl, yes.'

'Thanks for listening to me, John.'

'No problem, right, let's have another beer - let me see if my knee is ok.' John stood up fine. 'Looks like it's sorted, Carl, what are you having?'

'I'll try the Pentrich ale please, John.' John stood at the bar and his mobile rang it was Joni.

'John?'

'Hi, what's up?'

'Nothing, Rick said I could leave early and I wondered if you were about.'

'I'm at the Tow'd Man with Carl - get your walking gear and come up then you can stay at mine tonight if you want.'

Sad Man
Second in the series of the
John Gammon Peak District Crime Thrillers

'Ok, John, see you in a bit.'

It was 9.40pm when Joni arrived and sat down with Carl and John. Her first glass of cider hardly touched the sides; 'I was ready for that, John.'

'Have you been busy?'

'We were early on but with music on up here it died off about 8.30pm so Rick said I could leave.'

'Hey, Joni.'

'Hi Cindy, who are you out with?'

'Just a few of the girls, do you want to join us?'

'Sorry, Cindy, I'm with John and Carl.'

'Blimey, that gorgeous policeman, John Gammon?'

'Well, yeah, I have been seeing him for a few days now.'

'Good on yer, girl, wait until I tell the rest of them.'

'Who's that, Joni?'

'It's Cindy Swanky, she is such a laugh, John, we used to go out in a gang when Beth was alive.'

'I have some news for you, Joni, I have decided to buy Rita Butts's cottage.'

Sad Man
Second in the series of the
John Gammon Peak District Crime Thrillers

'Oh that's great, Carl, Beth would be so happy but please do me one favour - don't put your life on hold - you have to move on, Beth would have wanted it.'

'I won't, I promise.'

'Think I will set you up a date.'

'Not just yet, mate, give me a bit more time.'

'John, are you going to have a dance with me?'

'Sorry, Carol, I am having problems with my knee.'

'Any bloody excuse, you wimp.'

'Are you really, John?'

'Only a bit, Joni, but it was a good excuse.'

'You will be ok for tomorrow?'

'Yes, no problem.'

'Tell me where I am going!'

'You will see!'

'Don't tease, John Gammon.'

'Well, we are going to end up at Steve and Jo's for a coffee.'

Sad Man
Second in the series of the
John Gammon Peak District Crime Thrillers

'Sounds great, looking forward to seeing Jo's mansion - bet she has got it lovely. Where is it John?'

'It's in Monkash - you will be impressed, Joni, it really is outstanding.'

'I really can't wait, John.' The Wine Drinkers Leg Iron came back from a break and got straight into Hi Ho Silver Lining. 'Come on, John, I like this.' John didn't want to spoil Joni's fun but he hated this song with a vengeance so he grimaced his way through the song smiling politely at Joni.

It was 11.30pm when the group announced the last song for the night; a rendition of You Will Never Walk Alone. John thought it was a bit of an odd song to end with by such a rock chick band but how wrong was he - the floor was packed. Everyone held hands and danced, and it really ended the night on a high. Joni leaned forward and embraced John at the end. The whole pub was shouting for more but the band had finished. John thought the girls would go far; they were very talented.

'Shall we have one last drink before we go, Joni?'

'Fine by me but just a coke for me then I can drive.' John ordered the last drink and they sat down. It was very warm in the Tow'd Man, the ceilings were

Sad Man
Second in the series of the
John Gammon Peak District Crime Thrillers

very low and there were a lot of sweaty bodies in the pub. Lucy Amy Lucy came over.

'Its Joni Horalek, isn't it?'

'Yes, thought you hadn't recognised me.'

'Sorry, when I am on stage I am just focused, I don't look around or I get too nervous. My twin sister on the other hand has no nerves at all.' She whispered in Joni's ear, 'How is Carl? So sad about his girlfriend - Beth.'

'He is coping.'

'I heard he had left the police force.'

'No, he moved from Derby to Bixton. Oh, John, I'm sorry, this is Lucy Amy Lucy - a friend of Carl's.'

'Pleased to meet you, Lucy, I'm John Gammon.'

'Wow, you're that famous detective, aren't you?'

'Well don't know about famous, Lucy!'

'Well listen, I better help the band clear away, lovely to see you both.'

'You too, Lucy, enjoyed the night - you were brilliant. Are you about ready, John? I need to be fresh for our secret walk tomorrow.'

Sad Man
Second in the series of the
John Gammon Peak District Crime Thrillers

They eventually climbed into John's bed at 1.15am. John set the alarm for 8am and they both fell straight to sleep in each other's arms Joni with a smile on her face like a cat that had got the cream.

The alarm duly woke them both at 8.00am. John showered and made a coffee for them both while Joni was getting ready. They left the house and arrived at Daisy drop car park for the start of their walk.

'We will walk about four miles and then stop for some breakfast if you want, Joni?'

'I am in your hands today, Sir.'

'I like the sound of that.' The walk took them down the valley in to Monkash Dale. All the wild flowers were out and the valley was carpeted with so many different colours; it looked like they were walking through a rainbow. It was now just gone ten o clock when they came across a small wooden cabin with some picnic tables outside. On the chalkboard outside it said Karen and Jimmy Jigley welcome you too the Sloppy Quiche Cafe.

Inside there were seven tables all with white linen table clothes and in the middle of each table was a piece of pottery shaped like a beehive with a couple of bees on the lid. Inside those were cubes of white and brown sugar. The salt and vinegar pots were

Sad Man
Second in the series of the
John Gammon Peak District Crime Thrillers

shaped like two lorries; red and blue. 'This is lovely, John'.

A lady came over. 'My name is Karen and I will be your server today, welcome to our little café, what can I serve you both with today?'

'I'll have a black coffee.'

'And can I have a tea please?'

'Would you like some food? Everything you see on the chalkboard is available all day.'

'Could I have the Jigley Breakfast please?'

'And for you madam?'

'Could I have the spinach, feta and peppers omelette please?'

'Ok, so I have tea for the lady with an omelette and for you, Sir, black coffee and our very own Jigley Breakfast - you won't be disappointed.'

'Thank you,' and Karen took away the menus.

'How did you know about this place, John?'

'Just by chance - last night when I was at the bar I overheard Fred Kite from Pritwich saying to Denis that the two girls singing were Jimmy Jigley sisters. He has the trucks in Pritwich and his wife has the cafe in Monkash Dale and he was enthusing about how good Karen's quiches were or as Fred put it they were Legend!'

The drinks arrived and within minutes the food arrived too. 'Please enjoy, if you require a top up with your drinks or anything else, let me know - all top ups are free.' John's breakfast was massive; three slices of bacon, two large sausages, two eggs, fried bread, mushrooms, fried potatoes, beans and tomatoes; then Karen appeared with two thick cut slices of buttered toast.

Joni's omelette was big enough for three people. 'Wow, John this is incredible.' While they were eating, the cafe slowly filled up with walkers and by the time they were leaving it was full and you could see why. John went to the counter to pay.

'That will be £7.44 please.'

'Karen, that is the best breakfast I have ever had and Joni was so pleased with the omelette, please keep the change,' and John handed her a ten pound note.

'Well thank you, please call again.'

'Oh we will, Karen, that is a promise.'

They left the cafe and John took a right turn over a style, which led them down the Lamplight way passing the steps leading to Up the Steps Maggie's pub. 'This will always remind me of Beth - I remember her telling me about finding the pub and meeting Posh Pete Barrington for the first time.'

'It's very sad, Joni, and must be hard for you and Carl. It doesn't matter how much I am exposed to murders and killings and all the bad things I have to deal with in my job, it sadness me to say it still gives me a feeling of despondency when I see what people do to people.'

'That's probably good then, John, at least you have not become anesthetised to the real world.'

They had gone about two miles down Cowdale Dale when they took a left the view at this point was stunning. 'Just look at that, Joni, you can see Hittington from here, can you see the church steeple?'

'Oh yeah.'

'Well, we are about four miles from Monkash where we will rejoin Monkash Dale now so we should be at Steve and Jo's for about midday I guess.' As they walked down Monkash Dale, Joni held John's hand. John for some reason still wasn't sure about this - he knew he wasn't over Vicky Wills but he didn't know why. Joni was very pretty and was

Sad Man
Second in the series of the
John Gammon Peak District Crime Thrillers

great company. He knew he had to shake himself out of the yearning for Vicky.

John was spot on with the timings - it was ten past twelve when they were walking up the drive to Jo's mansion. 'Blimey, this is some place, John.'

'Wait until you get inside.'

Jo met them both at the front door. 'Steve has nipped to B&Q for paint but he should be back anytime, what are you having to drink? I have got most spirits, or some really nice Chablis, Joni?'

'I'll have Chablis if that's ok.'

'What about Mr Gammon?'

'Have you got any Vodka, Jo?'

'I've got Grey Goose, Stoli or Cracked Skull.'

'Oh heck, think I will miss on the Cracked Skull stuff, can I have a Stoli on the rocks?'

'I don't know how you drink it straight, John, it's like drinking paint thinners!'

'You get used to it, Jo.' John had just taken his first sip when the door opened and in came Steve with five tins of emulsion.

'She is a real slave driver, John.'

Sad Man
Second in the series of the
John Gammon Peak District Crime Thrillers

'You like it really, Stevie Boy.'

'Certainly do, don't I, Jo? Hey are you drinking my vodka?'

'We have saved you the Cracked Skull.'

'Typical of you, Porky, what a pussy.' Jo poured Steve a Cracked Skull with coke. The day carried on with Jo pouring the drinks, the lads slowly getting drunk and the girls in the giggly stage. It was late afternoon when Steve finally decided he needed the toilet. As he got off the chrome stool, he slipped and fell on the floor. Everyone rallied round trying to pick him up but Steve was a thick-set lad and he was just laughing and telling Jo how much he loved her. 'Get up you big lump.' They finally got Steve up and he staggered off to the bathroom bouncing of the walls as he went.

Jo pulled a cooked chicken out of the oven. She had buttered some farmhouse cobs earlier and had made a Greek salad. 'We better get some food or we all be as bad as Steve. Are you too stopping tonight? I have made a bed up.'

'If you don't mind, Jo, I left my car at Cowdale so it will be ok.'

The night carried on in the same vein; everyone was pretty much in a state by 10.00pm so John helped Steve to bed first for Jo, then Joni was quite wobbly so he took her to bed and said goodnight to Jo thanking her for a nice day.

John climbed in alongside Joni who looked as pretty as an angel with such a peaceful persona about her. He lay for maybe an hour trying to get Vicky out of his head and eventually he fell off to sleep. Joni woke John at 9am, 'Where are we John?'

'Can't you remember?'

'The last thing I remember was Steve falling of his stool in the kitchen, are we still at Jo's place?'

'Yes we stayed the night.'

'John, how beautiful is this room?' The four-poster bed had beautiful Green and cream drapes, which matched the bedding, and the ceiling had ornate plasterwork with cherubs playing little trumpets. The windows were small with leaded lights. Joni opened the window and the view took her breath away. The view looked over lush rolling hills. 'Years ago, John, this must have been some very rich person's place.'

'It has a lot of history - I know that Jo has found loads of stuff in the attics and has been researching it as well.'

Sad Man
Second in the series of the
John Gammon Peak District Crime Thrillers

Jo knocked on the bedroom door, 'I could hear you talking, do you want a bacon sandwich? Me and Steve are having one.'

'Great, we will be down in a minute.'

'If you want a shower there are fresh towels in your en suite.'

'Lovely, Jo, thank you.' Joni showered first before John, then they both went down for the sandwich. Steve looked dreadful.

John gave him a customary slap on the back, 'What's up you, pussy?' and he laughed.

'Ok, you win, Porky, just let me die here with my bacon sandwich. I never learn, do I, Porky, you always get me in a mess!'

'Why does he call you Porky, John?'

'Gammon?'

'Oh yeah, silly me.'

'He has always called me Porky from the first day we sat together at junior school - that was my nickname and his was Offside.'

'Blimey, you two known each other that long?'

'Always been best buddies haven't we, Steve?'

Sad Man
Second in the series of the
John Gammon Peak District Crime Thrillers

'Who put the brass band playing in my flippin' head - have we got anything for a banging headache, Jo?'

'Here, try these Aspirin.'

'Thanks,' Steve let out a loud groan, 'I hate taking tablets.'

'Then you should not drink with the big misters then, Offside.'

'Bollocks, Porky,' and they both laughed.

'Are they always like this, Jo?'

'As long as I have known them! Do you feel up to a tour, Joni?'

'Wouldn't miss it for anything - it is so beautiful, Jo.'

'Let's leave the boys watching last night's football while I show you round. I have done a picture album of the house; before and after.'

'Brilliant, what a great idea, Jo.'

'Ok, so this was the kitchen before - as you can see it was very old fashioned, I had an almighty fight with the listed building agency - they wanted me to keep it as was!'

'Can they do that, Jo?'

Sad Man
Second in the series of the
John Gammon Peak District Crime Thrillers

'Well, externally I can't really change anything but internally I can as long as they feel I am doing it right.'

'This is the most magnificent kitchen I think I have ever been in.'

'Well I quite like cooking so I have made sure I have everything at hand. Just off here is the walk-in pantry. I did keep the salting slabs and the beam with the hooks. They used to salt pigs in here then hang them up. Next is the dining room.'

'Wow, just wow, Jo, how beautiful.' Jo had bought an oak table that could seat sixteen people. The chairs were also oak with crusader crosses embellished in the backrests and they had cream leather seats. The walls were in a red flock paper with an oak dado rail running all round the room. There was a magnificent chandelier hanging over the table the like of which you see in country mansions. The curtains were a beautiful cream colour with Peacocks adorning them.

'Now follow me, my lady,' and she laughed.

'Jo, I feel like a lady, what a fabulous house.' They climbed the old oak staircase where halfway up there was picture window perfectly framing the old flourmill in the dale at Monkash like a Constable painting. Jo carried on with the tour then came back to find the boys watching a re-run of the 1968 European Cup Final between Manchester United and Benfica.

'So what do you think of Jo's Aunty Abigail's legacy, Joni?'

'I'm lost for words, Steve, it is absolutely fabulous.'

'It's all down to Jo - she has done all the interior design.'

'Yeah but without you, Steve, I could not have got half of it done.'

'Ok, you two, less of the appreciation society - can one of you drop me for my car? I need to go in to work.'

'Yeah, no problem, I'll run you to Cowdale.'

'Sorry about this Joni.'

'I understand, John, I have work as well - we have a badger set on Micklock Moor that we are trying to protect.'

'You be careful up there, Joni.'

'Its ok, Bob Watson the lead Park Ranger will be with me today.'

Sad Man
Second in the series of the
John Gammon Peak District Crime Thrillers

John picked up his car and thanked Steve for a nice day then dropped Joni off for her car. He arrived at Bixton and was met by Scooper. 'Sir, something has happened that is dreadful.'

'What, exactly?'

'Cristos Minolis has committed suicide in the holding cell. He left a note blaming you for everything. The family are here and they are baying for blood, Sir.'

'How did he commit the suicide?'

'He ripped a hand towel in two then stood on the bed with it attached to the bars and just jumped off and snapped his neck.'

'Bloody hell, Scooper, this is all I need.'

'Chief Constable wants to see you in her office straight away.'

Gammon walked past the desk Sergeant's desk. There were a couple of Minolis family there who started shouting 'killer' at him. Gammon carried on but the abuse was affecting him. Gammon felt quite nervous when he knocked on Wills's door. 'Come in.' Gammon entered the office to find Sergeant Hanney sat in one of the chairs. 'Sergeant Hanney, just run through the events leading up to Mr Minolis's suicide.'

Sad Man
Second in the series of the
John Gammon Peak District Crime Thrillers

'I came on shift at 11pm, Ma'am. PC Di Trimble had done the day shift so we went through what had happened and she said Minolis was brought in last night under instruction from Superintendent Gammon and that he was to be held for forty-eight hours and he would interview Monday morning.'

'How did Trimble describe Mr Minolis's state of mind?'

'She wrote in the log that he was very abusive and that he stated he would kill Gammon for ruining his life. He kept saying he had nothing, no wife; no children; no family and no job all, because of Gammon.'

'So what time did you find him?'

'I always check on anybody brought in once every two hours but if I think they have been drinking or are upset I make that every hour.'

'Why was there a hand towel in the cell?'

'We ran out of paper towels, Ma'am.'

'And is this normal practice, Sergeant?'

'I can only speak for my shift but this is the first time I have known it.'

'Did you give him the towel?'

Sad Man
Second in the series of the
John Gammon Peak District Crime Thrillers

'No, Ma'am.'

'So I can conclude from that, Sergeant, that PC Trimble put the towel there.'

'I guess so, Ma'am.'

'Ok, Sergeant, thank you.' Hanney left the office. 'John, there is going to be a shitstorm about this.'

'I don't know what to say.'

'Had you been hassling this guy?'

'No, not at all, what basically happened was - he was the taxi driver that came on strong to one of the girls that had been murdered so in the course of the investigation we had to go to his place of work and question him.'

'So what was the guy on about you ruining his life?'

'Apparently his father found out, not from the police I might add, so he cut him out of the will and sacked him. His wife left him and it was just a mess but all his own doing, Vicky. Anyway, I called to see Joni in the Wobbly Man and he was in there and had been telling everyone he was going to kill me and that he had a gun. So I did the sensible thing and arrested him. I told them at the station to hold him until Monday when I would charge him. I also

Sad Man
Second in the series of the
John Gammon Peak District Crime Thrillers

thought it was a good opportunity to get a search warrant on his house and car, Vicky.'

'Ok, John, I knew you would have all the angles covered. I will handle it from here.'

'Ok thanks.'

John made his way to the door when Vicky said, 'Is it serious then with this Joni girl?'

'Why do you ask, Vicky?'

'Oh nothing, thanks, John.' John thought it strange she should ask this question when she had made it plain she was in a relationship - was she playing with his emotions he wondered.

Gammon pulled the team together in the incident room. 'First of all, thank goodness we have not had any more incidents. Evans, any news on Tink?'

'No sign of him, Sir, we have checked his phone records and his bank account - he hasn't used his mobile and he hasn't used his debit or credit cards. He has just disappeared since that night.'

'Do you think the parents have helped him get away?'

'My opinion, for what its worth, I think Lund is involved.'

Sad Man
Second in the series of the
John Gammon Peak District Crime Thrillers

'Why, Scooper?'

'There are a lot of dodgy things going on in that pub that me and Inspector Smarty have seen a lot of over the last few weeks.'

'I think they may have done away with him - no witness, no trial, Sir.'

'You may be correct, Smarty, but your two's cover is blown now.'

'What about bugging the pub?'

'Not sure we can stack up a case for it - Lund is too clever, he knows how things work and I have always thought he has somebody on the inside.'

'Yes, Milton.'

'I knew of Lund when I was in Rapid Response in Derby - the detectives there have been after this guy and his henchmen since the beginning of time. He is very clever - he never leaves himself exposed where you can nail him.'

'Does he know you, Carl?'

'No, Sir.'

'I am thinking, if Chief Constable Wills will let us run with this, about getting somebody inside - that's the only way we will get him - would you be up for that?'

'Most certainly, Sir.'

'Ok, Milton, I will let you know later today after I have spoken with the powers that be. Ok, keep fishing, everyone, I want Tink found and I want Jim Reynolds watched very closely.' They broke from the incident room and Inspector Scooper asked Gammon for a quiet word.

'What's the problem, Scooper?'

'Not so much of a problem, Sir, just I was speaking with my Mum at the weekend and, please don't think I was discussing police business, but she asked me how the Micklock Moor case was going. I said ok, we have a few suspects but nothing concrete. She asked me if we had interviewed Meredith Alison.'

'Did your Mum know her?'

'She said she was older than her but she remembers that she was always odd. My grandfather owned some of the land near the Alison's house and they eventually sold it to Mr Alison so my Mum would have played up there as a chlld.

Sad Man
Second in the series of the
John Gammon Peak District Crime Thrillers

'Anyway, Sir, Mum said she was sure that Meredith Alison had a baby - a boy but rumour was it was adopted straight away because of the shame in those days.'

'Are you thinking what I am thinking, Scooper, that he may live with her and putting two and two together he would be close to the scene of all these rapes and the murder?'

'That's exactly what I thought, Sir.'

'Come on, Scooper,' lets visit Miss Alison.

Gammon and Scooper drove to the imposing house on Micklock Moor. They walked up the drive and went round the back to the kitchen door. Gammon knocked loudly; he could hear people speaking inside. Eventually, after a few heavy knocks on the door, Meredith Alison opened the kitchen door just wide enough so that she could see who had been knocking. 'What do you want again? How many times have I told you - I don't know anything else.'

'We are here on a different matter, Miss Alison.'

'I have no time for this, go away,' and she attempted to shut the door but Gammon put his foot in the way.

'We can either speak casually here or I can take you down to the station, Miss Alison.' After a few seconds, she took the chain off the door and let them into the kitchen.

They sat at the kitchen table and started to ask Miss Alison some questions. 'Can you tell me, Miss Alison, have you ever been married?'

'Why do you ask? It's nothing to do with you.'

'Have you got any children? Before you answer this, Miss Alison, think very hard and long before you answer this - we are investigating a rape and murder case, Miss Alison.'

She looked at Gammon with the eyes of Medusa. 'I will say it again - it's nothing to do with you but I have never been married and nor would I want to be. And the second question - the answer to that is no also.'

At this point Scooper asked if she could use the toilet; it was basically an excuse to have snoop around upstairs. She left Gammon sparring with Miss Alison. Climbing the stairs, Scooper noticed that the house smelt of damp and that the wallpaper was coming off the walls. The chandeliers that been grand once were desperately in need of a clean.

She quietly walked across the floor with all the boards creaking - it really was a scary place - until she came across what looked like Miss Alison's

Sad Man
Second in the series of the
John Gammon Peak District Crime Thrillers

bedroom. At the side of the bed was a picture of a baby. Scooper picked up the picture and on the back it said 'January 1957 my Christopher'. She heard Miss Alison coming upstairs and just managed to get to the bathroom. 'What are you doing in there, young lady?'

'Just finished,' and Scooper flushed the toilet chain and pretended to wash her hands. She opened the door and Miss Alison was looking at her in a menacing way.

'Get down my stairs now, you have no right to walk around my house.'

'I'm sorry but I needed the toilet.'

'Ok, Miss Alison, we will be in touch if we need to speak anymore.'

'Don't see that I can help you any further so I would be grateful if you left me alone.'

'Good day, Miss Alison.' Scooper and Gammon walked down the drive and climbed into Gammon's car. 'Something isn't right with that woman, Inspector.'

'I know, Sir, I took the liberty of having a snoop around in what I thought was her bedroom; I found a picture of a little boy and on the back it said

Sad Man
Second in the series of the
John Gammon Peak District Crime Thrillers

'January 1957 my Christopher', the boy looked about three years old.'

'Right, I will drop you in Bixton at Births, Deaths and Marriages. Get Evans to pick you up once you have found if anything was registered under Miss Alison's name, Scooper.'

'I will, then see you this afternoon for briefing.' Gammon left Scooper at Bixton registry office and decided to have a longer chat with his Mum about Miss Alison.

'Hey, John, this is a lovely surprise.'

'Hi, Mum, can I have a coffee? Why, of course, John, and what about a raspberry coconut scone? They have just come out of the oven.'

'You spoil me, Mum.' John sat at the big farmhouse kitchen table and his mother duly arrived with a coffee and a hot scone. 'Mum, I wanted to know if you can remember anything about Miss Alison and the baby. She denies ever having any children.'

'Well it was like this; Meredith Alison was a lovely girl and when we were very small I used to play with her because we would be at the land that surrounded her house. When she was nine, her father sent her away to Public school - somewhere in Oxfordshire, I think, John. I never saw her much after that but if I did see her she had become very introverted and always seemed so unhappy. She must have hated the school but her father was a very nasty man and believed that children should be seen but not heard.

'Meredith is a little older than me, I am guessing she would be about seventy-three now. Nobody really knows what happened but from my recollection, Meredith became pregnant by the gardener of the school she was at and I believe she had a boy but I think her father made her give the baby up for adoption.'

'I heard it was her father's accountant, Mum?'

'John, this is only hearsay and you know how people embellish the truth in these villages. All I know is she never returned to school and she has lived at that house ever since. Her father died three years later and her mother had died many years before so she was left on her own. She shunned everybody; the only time she is seen in Micklock is on market day when she does her shopping once a week. I have not seen her but they say she dresses like she is in permanent mourning for something. Why do you want to know all this, John? Is she in trouble?'

'Not sure yet, Mum, I just have a hunch that's all. I may be way off line. Listen, Mum, thanks for your help, I need to get back to the station. Did I tell you that Uncle Graham is coming to see me tomorrow? Don't know what it's about... I will give you a call tomorrow night, Mum.'

'Ok, son, lovely to see you.'

John arrived back at the station and was immediately summoned to Vicky Wills's office. 'John, this shit has hit the fan over Cristos Minolis - we have the Police Complaints Commission coming in tomorrow and they want to interview you, PC Trimble, Sergeant Hanney and myself - apparently the story will run in the nationals tomorrow, John.'

'Shit, that's not good.'

'Nothing we can do, John, we will just have to ride the storm I guess.'

'Ok, Vicky, I have a meeting in the incident room if you want to attend.'

'Sorry, John, this business is taking up all my time.'

'Understand, Vicky.'

Gammon gathered all the officers in the incident room. 'Scooper, what have you found out?'

'There was a baby boy registered as Christopher Alison, Father unknown, on January 1957.'

Sad Man
Second in the series of the
John Gammon Peak District Crime Thrillers

'Great, well done, Scooper. Do you remember that Eric Stein said Miss Alison was batty and that she talked to herself and that he had heard voices? My hunch is that her son lives with her!'

'Do you think he is involved in the rapes and murders, Sir?'

'I certainly think he knows something about them, Sergeant Milton.'

'Right. Evans, I want a warrant to search the Alison house for tomorrow.'

'Ok, Sir, will sort it.'

'Where are we on the Tink disappearance?'

'Still no sign, Sir.'

'Put a watch on the Tink household - you can do that Trimble. Any more news on Lund, Smarty?'

'Nothing, Sir, he appears to have gone to ground - he is certainly keeping a low profile.'

'What about his henchmen?'

'Not seen any of them since Tink disappeared, Sir.'

'Ok, we all know what we are doing. Tomorrow afternoon the Police Complaints Commission will be here and they wish to speak with you, Trimble,

Sad Man
Second in the series of the
John Gammon Peak District Crime Thrillers

as well as Hanney so please be available. That's all, thanks.'

John called it a day and as he climbed in his car he called Joni. 'Hi John, what are you on with?'

'Just finished work and wondered if you fancy a drink with me at The Spinning Wheel at Swinster.'

'Yeah, that would be nice.'

'Well, drive to my house and we can have a taxi.'

'Bit presumptuous there, Mr Gammon, who said I was staying the night?'

'Oh, Joni, sorry I wasn't meaning anything.'

'I am only joking, of course I want to stay the night.'

'Ok, see you in about half an hour.' John drove back to the cottage, shaved and showered. He was dressed and ready by the time Joni arrived.

As the taxi pulled into the Spinning Jenny, John could see Bob and Cheryl looking as if they were in a heated discussion. 'Hi you two.'

'Hello John, Joni.'

Joni and John carried on into the pub. 'Hey John, how are you both?'

Sad Man
Second in the series of the
John Gammon Peak District Crime Thrillers

'Good thanks, Doreen, what's up with Bob and Cheryl?'

'Something and nothing - we are having a race-day to York and Bob said they would both go but Cheryl said she didn't want to go because Bob would get too much to drink and be larey, as she put it, so they went outside to discuss it. My money is on Cheryl.'

'I disagree, Doreen, Bob will win the day.'

Just then they came back in all smiles. 'Well, you two, are you coming or not?'

'Yes we are, Doreen,' Bob said in a very 'I'm the boss' tone. 'Good, that's that sorted then.'

Joni leaned over to Cheryl and asked how Bob got her to change her mind. 'It's all tactics, Joni, he promised to behave and said he would buy me a handbag I had seen in Bags and Hats in Micklock.'

'Well done, mate, must remember that tactic!'

'Are you two eating tonight, John?'

'Yes please, Doreen.'

'So what do you fancy?'

'Can I have the Whitby Cod with new potatoes and mushy peas please, Doreen?'

Sad Man
Second in the series of the
John Gammon Peak District Crime Thrillers

'You certainly can, Joni. Now what about John?'

'I'm going to try the meatloaf wrapped in bacon with baby roast potatoes and a medley of veg please, Doreen.'

'You will like that, John, chef made it fresh today.' A couple of drinks and their meals came out. John took his first mouthful when his mobile rang.

'Sorry, Joni, I will have to take this. Hi, Vicky, you ok?'

'There has been another rape, John, same person we believe. Can you come in?'

'Yes, no problem, Vicky.' John felt he had to oblige as Vicky was under a lot of pressure because of the Minolis case. 'Joni, I am going to have to leave this - I am needed at work. I'll get a taxi back to pick my car up and arrange for him to pick you up later.'

'Ok, John, I will see you later then.' John could hear the disappointment in Joni's voice but he had no option. The taxi picked John up and he drove his car to Bixton. It was 8.40pm when John sat down in the interview room with the young girl that had claimed rape. She was very pale and very upset. She had an older guy with her that John assumed was her father.

Sad Man
Second in the series of the
John Gammon Peak District Crime Thrillers

'I'm Superintendent John Gammon, this is Sergeant Milton, now, in your own time explain to me what has happened please. Let's start with your name.'

'Jane Wells.'

The man said, 'I'm Jane's father, Don Wells.'

'Ok if I call you Jane and Don?'

They both nodded.

'Just lead me through the night's events please, Jane.'

'I have college three nights a week - I am studying to be dentist. I left Bixton College at the normal time and walked across town to catch the bus home.'

'Where is home, Jane?'

'I live in Cowdale. I was a little late for the bus because my friend Sarah had been telling me about a concert she had been to on Saturday to see a band called Fallout Boy - they are touring at the moment and she was telling me she had been on stage. I hadn't realised the time so I had to run across town, as the last bus was 8.55pm. I knew I was late so I took a short cut.'

'Just hold it there, Jane, this happened when?'

Sad Man
Second in the series of the
John Gammon Peak District Crime Thrillers

'Last night.'

'Why did you not report it last night?'

'That's my fault, Mr Gammon, I didn't know what to do - there is only me and Jane. Jane's Mum died three years ago. I think I was frightened that if it got out then my daughter's life would be ruined.' At this Jane broke down sobbing uncontrollably.

'Take a minute, Jane. All that matters is you are here now. Shall we try again, Jane?'

'I walked across the park, it was quite dimly lit and from nowhere the man grabbed me. I tried to fight him off - I used to do Judo but I couldn't get hold of him - he had something round his coat that cut me every time I tried to grab him. He kept laughing; it was awful. The next thing I knew he had some cloth to my mouth and the next thing I remember is waking up with this thing on top of me. It was dark but I knew I was in some wet ground. I tried to struggle but again could not get hold of him then he hit me really hard and I blacked out. When I came round he had gone. I staggered across two muddy fields and found the road. I flagged down a car and lucky for me it was a woman who lived in Cowdale and she got me home.'

'Can you describe your attacker?'

Sad Man
Second in the series of the
John Gammon Peak District Crime Thrillers

'He was about six feet two, he wore a black ski mask which had red lips. His coat was a light coloured raincoat - like something you see those detectives wearing in old films on the telly.'

'Please roll your sleeves up, Jane.'

As Gammon thought - the exact same markings as the other rape victims. 'Ok, Jane, well thank you for being so brave, the doctor will now give you a full examination.'

The doctor took Jane away and Gammon had a few minutes with Don Wells. 'Does Jane go out much on her own, Don?'

'She is a normal eighteen year old, Mr Gammon, but she is studying hard and she is very focused on what she wants out of life - I just hope this doesn't affect those dreams.'

'I'm sure she will recover, Don. Time is a great healer.'

'I am just praying he hasn't raped her, Mr Gammon.'

'I'll get the desk Sergeant to get you a cup of tea. Milk and sugar?'

'Just milk please, Mr Gammon.' Gammon felt for Don Wells; it would not have been easy bringing a young girl up on his own and she seemed a very level-headed young lady.

After almost an hour, Jane came back and the doctor called Gammon aside. 'Not good, I am afraid there has been sexual intercourse and I don't think from looking at the bruising that it was consensual. One shining light, though, John, I did find some semen that you may be able to get a DNA result from.'

'Brilliant, Doc, you are my hero.'

John went back into the room with Jane and Don Wells. 'Not good news, I am afraid it does look like you have been raped.' Jane broke down and her father had tears rolling down his cheeks.

'I will kill the bastard if you ever get him, Mr Gammon.'

'We will get him, Mr Wells, he is making too many slip ups to stay under the radar much longer. Look, you need to go home, if you want a counsellor I can arrange that and I would advise you do in the circumstances.' Jane nodded in agreement. 'Are you ok to drive, Mr Wells?

'Yes, thank you.'

Sad Man
Second in the series of the
John Gammon Peak District Crime Thrillers

'Ok, I will be in touch. Sergeant, contact the counselling department and arrange for somebody to visit Jane.'

'Ok, Sir.'

Jane and her father left and Gammon called Joni. 'Are you home yet?'

'No, John, I cancelled the taxi and said I would call him later if I need him. I'm sat with Bob, Cheryl, Jackie, Tony, Rita and Carol. There is a guy playing all the Beatles music, just some random guy who was passing - he calls himself the travelling Minstrel.'

'Ok well I will come back up and see you in a bit.' John was just leaving the station and he noticed Vicky Wills stood by her car on the phone but clearly upset. John wandered over and Vicky came off the phone.

'Oh, John, what a mess.'

'Get in the car, Vicky, so we can talk. What's the matter? This is not like you.'

'My relationship is over. I have had the deputy Home secretary on the phone tearing a real strip off me; my career isn't looking too rosy at the minute. You get off, John, I'm sure you have better things to do than listen to my problems.'

Sad Man
Second in the series of the
John Gammon Peak District Crime Thrillers

'Vicky, don't treat me like a stranger, you know I care about you.   Let's have a quick drink somewhere.'

'Ok, what about the Hideaway on the A515?'

'Suits me, see you there.' John's heart was racing - he had never got over Vicky.   He totally forgot about Joni.

The little pub just off the A515 was pretty much empty.   It had a food reputation but wasn't a drinker's pub because of its location. John ordered a pint of Green Goblin and a Gin and tonic for Vicky and they sat in a corner. 'So what's the problem?'

'Jeremy is taking a post in Saudi Arabia with the Petro Chemical Company he works for so really that has killed the relationship and to be honest I think he was pleased when I said it was over.'

'First things first you had a relationship with somebody called Jeremy?' and they both laughed - it was like old times and John had missed that.

'Then I have all this crap at work.'

'It wasn't your fault, Vicky.'

'Try telling that to Lord Stathon, Deputy Home Secretary - he is not a happy bunny.'

Sad Man
Second in the series of the
John Gammon Peak District Crime Thrillers

'What would he know about policing?'

'If the towel had not been there, he could not have hung himself and how can I ruin and officer like Di Trimble's career? They need a scapegoat John.'

'Vicky, let's see how tomorrow goes first.'

'That's what I like about you, John, you are always positive. Thanks John, that's cheered me up, I best get on my way.'

'Oh shit, I forgot I am supposed to be seeing Joni at the Spinning Jenny an hour ago.'

'Well we don't want to let Joni down now do we,' Vicky said in a condescending voice. John just smiled and pecked her on the cheek. He drove as fast as he could to the Spinning Jenny.

When he walked in Kev said, 'I'm sorry, John, we have called last orders.'

'No problem, Kev, just picking Joni up.' Luckily Joni was a bit worse for wear so had lost all track of time and did not realise that John had said he was on his way. 'Come on then, let's have you. What have you done to her Cheryl?'

'She was drinking with the big misters tonight, John. Shelley was in also.'

Sad Man
Second in the series of the
John Gammon Peak District Crime Thrillers

'Oh heck, poor Joni.'

As soon as they arrived back at John's cottage he put Joni straight to bed then sat downstairs with a coffee. He couldn't get Vicky out of his mind, *why was she being condescending about Joni if she wasn't interested in their relationship?* Typical women, he thought he would never understand them.

Joni woke about 4.30am and came downstairs for a glass of water. John was fast asleep in the armchair next to the Rayburn. 'John, you ok?'

John woke up in a startled state. 'John my head is banging, I don't how Shelley can drink so much.'

'Practice, Joni, why are you down here? I thought I would let you get off to sleep then come up but I must have dozed off.'

'Come on let's go back to bed and cuddle up.' They were both soon asleep again and didn't stir again until the alarm went over at 8.00am.

'Do you want some breakfast Joni?'

'Just a slice off toast will be fine.'

'Ok, you shower, I'll have my breakfast and pop you some toast in then I can get ready for work.' Joni went off to shower and John came downstairs and made some fresh coffee. He cut some brown wholemeal bread and put four slices in the toaster; he popped two down for himself but was waiting for Joni to arrive before toasting her slices. 'Listen, I am going to have to get off for work, just put the key under the plant pot and I will give you a call later on, Joni.'

'Ok thanks, John, I only work half a day today so I'm not in any rush.'

John left the cottage. The climb out of Hittington-on-the Dale was glorious; the sun was shining and the little lambs were playing in the field - *this place really is God's garden,* a saying John's Dad would say to him and Adam when they were little boys.

Gammon strode into Bixton station like a man on a mission. 'Sergeant Hanney, ensure the holding cells are at the standard they should be - I don't want the investigating officers finding pens and such like in those cells - I am making this your responsibility, are we clear?'

'Yes, Sir, I'll take care of it.'

'Evans, get everyone in the incident room by 9.15am.'

'Ok, Sir.' John climbed the stairs to his office but noticed Vicky's office was empty. He grabbed a coffee out of the vending machine and sat down to contemplate how he was going to get this investigation back on track. His mobile rang. 'John, its Vicky, you will have to deal with the Police Complaints people - I have been summoned to London to meet Lord Stathon for lunch at the Criterion in Leicester Square.'

'Is it bad, Vicky?'

'I honestly don't know - he didn't arrange it with me, it was his PA.'

'Well, don't worry about here, I can sort that, you have enough on your plate.'

'John, I really appreciate your support, I hope you didn't get in trouble with your girlfriend last night.'

'No everything's ok.'

'Ok, John, speak later.'

Again John thought it a little odd but who was he to judge; with women he really didn't have a clue. It was 9.15am and time for the meeting in the incident room. John strode in purposefully. 'Everyone here, Evans?'

'Just Inspector Scooper missing, Sir.'

'Is she coming?'

Sad Man
Second in the series of the
John Gammon Peak District Crime Thrillers

'She rung to say she was running late.' Just then the door opened and Scooper came in offering her apologises.

'I don't like lateness, Inspector, please remember that.' Scooper felt dreadful, everyone was looking at her. 'Right, let's move on.' John put the name of Jane Wells on the incident board. 'Let's see what, if any, connections we have. First victim, Dana Bryant, abducted from Bixton after a night out with friends - she was raped – connection we have:

'Spoken to Jim Reynolds; this guy has a temper and has knocked Mrs Bryant about, Dana's mother. Also, the now deceased, Cristos Minolis - think we can count him out now. Victim number two - Milan Peterson, not much connecting this young lady with anyone at the moment. Suzy Warner the third victim and the only one murdered so far. It appears that Suzy was a drug user. Her boyfriend Mark Anthony Tink as you are all aware is on the run. Suzy Warner did have a chance meeting with both the deceased taxi driver and Jim Reynolds. I also believe Mark Anthony Tink is possibly dealing for Brian Lund. Victim four Lara Bennett - as yet nothing to ascertain that she has had any contact with Jim Reynolds or Tink. Victim number five Mary Denham - again nothing to suggest she has met Jim Reynolds or Tink. Victim six Mary Wells – again, no obvious connection to suspects. One thing they all have in common is the description of

Sad Man
Second in the series of the
John Gammon Peak District Crime Thrillers

the attacker is consistent. They all also have severe lacerations on their arms where they struggled with this guy. Ok, everyone, thoughts please.'

Scooper said, 'I think this Jim Reynolds guy is connected in some way.'

'Evans?'

'I'm with Scooper on this.'

'Anyone else agree with these two?'

'I do, Sir.'

'Ok, Trimble.'

'Me also, Sir.'

'Ok, Bannon.'

'What about you Bradbury?'

'To be honest, Sir, I thought it was the taxi driver.'

'So did I.'

'Ok, so Bradbury and Smarty are the lame ducks on this one! Milton what about you?'

'I'm not sure, Sir, but there is something strange about Miss Alison.'

Sad Man
Second in the series of the
John Gammon Peak District Crime Thrillers

'What you think she is raping people?' The whole incident room erupted in laughter.

'No, Sir, just everything seems to revolve around that area and that is the only house for miles.'

'Well, actually, Milton, you get my vote - that's why I want you to come on the warrant to search the house. Smarty, Scooper, Bannon and Trimble - you come with me and Milton. Evans and Bradbury, see if we can get thing sorted on the Tink problem.

'Right, everyone, on this house search I want to take this in a kindly manner; she is an old lady and the last thing this force needs is her having a heart attack or something. Ok, let's go, I will issue the warrant but first I want to speak with her and Scooper so you all wait in the cars until I give you the signal.'

They arrived at the old house on Micklock Moor. John and Scooper went round to the back door and knocked. 'Good morning, Miss Alison.'

'What do you want? This is becoming a little tedious, Mr Gammon.'

'I think we need a word, Miss Alison, either here or down at the station.'

Sad Man
Second in the series of the
John Gammon Peak District Crime Thrillers

'I have done nothing wrong; my father was a benefactor of Micklock and the surrounding villages.'

'That's as maybe, Miss Alison, but I need to speak with you.'

'Come in, then. What is this all about?'

'Previously, I asked you if you had ever had any family and you said no, is that correct?'

'Absolutely correct.'

'Well, can you explain to me and Inspector Scooper why this birth certificate would show your name?' Gammon produced a copy of the birth certificate. Miss Alison pulled a lace handkerchief from up her sleeve and started to cry. 'This is your boy, Miss Alison?' She nodded in agreement. 'Why did you lie to us? Are you protecting him in some way? Is he connected with these dreadful events that have occurred up here on the moor?'

Miss Alison regained her composure. 'I lied because it is a family secret and not something my father would allow me, or anyone, to speak off. Christopher was born and christened, then within two days of the birth he was then taken from me and put up for adoption. My father registered the birth at Bixton, not at Micklock, because he didn't want people knowing.'

Sad Man
Second in the series of the
John Gammon Peak District Crime Thrillers

'So, Miss Alison, where is Christopher now?'

'I never saw him again.'

'Is that the truth? Think carefully before you answer - this is a murder investigation, Miss Alison, and if you are lying to me, you could be charged with being an accessory to the murder.'

'I told you, I have never seen him since.'

'Your gardener has told us he has heard you arguing with somebody.'

'He should not be nosy. I like quiz programmes on the radio and I say the answers - that is what he would have heard.'

'Miss Alison, I am sorry to have to do this,' and Gammon produced the search warrant.

She broke down again, 'Why are you doing this to me?'

'Scooper, you sit with Miss Alison.' Gammon got up and signalled to the rest of the police waiting for the signal. They had been told to be careful. They crawled all over the house and found a pair of men's cream coloured trousers in a wash basket. 'Whose are these, Miss Alison?'

'They were my father's.'

Sad Man
Second in the series of the
John Gammon Peak District Crime Thrillers

'We will have to take these for forensics. Why were they in the wash basket?'

'I had just washed them. I know this sounds silly but I snuggle up to them at night - it's all I have left of Daddy.'

'Ok, everyone done? Outside been done?'

'All done, Sir.'

'I will be in touch, Miss Alison.

'Not sure if I am right or not, Scooper, but this just does not add up. I was convinced that she was lodging her son, yet they found nothing, how can that be?'

'Maybe he was there but left.'

'You would leave some small trail I am sure. Let's go and speak with Eric Stein again.'

Gammon pulled up outside the Poor House in Swinster - Stein's home. Stein was attending his garden. 'Nice show of flowers, Mr Stein.'

'What do you lot want? Don't you ever leave an innocent man alone?'

'Just a few words, unless you would like us to take you to Bixton station for this chat, Eric?'

Sad Man
Second in the series of the
John Gammon Peak District Crime Thrillers

'No, here will be fine.'

'As a matter of interest, where were you when our latest victim was raped, Eric?'

'Look, I have told you - every night I have the same routine which always involves a few cans and me falling asleep in the chair, so no, I don't have anybody who can vouch for me as I live alone. Now either charge me or leave me a damn well alone.'

'No need for the aggression, Eric, we are just here to ask you a few questions. In your capacity as gardener at Miss Alison's, have you ever seen a man at the house, in the sheds or anywhere else?'

'No, never. Hang on a minute though, a couple of year back I went to get my wages - Miss Alison pays me cash in hand - I knocked on the door and I was sure I saw a big guy leaving the kitchen. I did say to Miss Alison 'have you got yourself a bit of company' and she gave me short sharp rebuke and told me I was the gardener and to keep my nose out of her business.'

'Did you ever see the man again?'

'I can't swear it was a man, but man or woman they were on the big side.'

'How was the person dressed?'

Sad Man
Second in the series of the
John Gammon Peak District Crime Thrillers

'I think they had cream coloured slacks on - that's what made me think it was a man, but to be honest, I can't remember.'

'Ok, Eric, well thanks for your time, don't leave the country.'

'Comedian as well as a policeman, hey? Like I can afford to go abroad!'

Gammon and Scooper left Stein to his dahlias and they drove back to Bixton. 'Bit of a coincidence about the cream slacks, Sir.'

'Not sure if Stein is a credible witness - he would say anything if it got him off the hook. I'm going to drop you at the station, Scooper, and call it a day.'

'Ok, Sir, got anything planned tonight?' Scooper was hoping Gammon might ask if she wanted a drink with him but he didn't take the bait.

'Nothing really, Sandra, just have a couple on the way home - think I might call in at Up the Steps Maggie's.'

Scooper saw her chance, 'Would you mind if I joined you?'

'No follow me up, Sandra.' Gammon arrived first; this was a quaint little pub, probably one of John's favourites. The floors were all stone flags, it was all

Sad Man
Second in the series of the
John Gammon Peak District Crime Thrillers

wooden beams and leaded windows; a real gem of a place.

'Can I help you, Sir?' the barmaid asked.

'Yes, can I have a pint of Cockles Shirt lifter please?'

'Certainly.'

Just then Sandra arrived. 'What are you having Sandra?'

'Glass of Rosé wine please.'

The barmaid turned round, 'I know that voice anywhere - how's Sandra?'

'Blimey, if it's not Maria McCready! How are you?' John just stood in amazement while the two girls swapped reasons for being there. Once finished Sandra and John sat in a window seat.

'Old friend, Sandra?'

'Very much so, Sir.'

'Call me John, Sandra, we are off duty.'

'Sorry, John. Maria and I went to Junior School together at Pritwich but we lost touch when I was sent away to private school.'

Sad Man
Second in the series of the
John Gammon Peak District Crime Thrillers

'That's a shame.'

'Yeah, I heard she had joined the RAF and married a pilot, which apparently was correct. Her Mum used to clean for my Mum at the hall until she died about four years ago. That was dreadful too, John, she was hit by a bus on a level crossing in Micklock. She really is a nice girl. Can I tell you something? I hope you won't be mad at me...'

'Of course, fire away, Sandra.'

'The other day, Di Trimble said to me that she thought you were a sad man - are you sad, John?'

'No, I don't think so, is that how I appear?'

'Sometimes, but you have been through an awful lot lately.'

'I guess it takes a toll on you and you don't realise Sandra. So how is your love life, Miss Scooper?'

'Pretty much nothing happening on that front - too much involved in my job, I guess.'

'Sandra, you have to have a life out of the job - you are doing it all wrong.' Sandra had thrown down the bait and was just waiting for John to bite but she didn't get the answer she expected. 'What about Sergeant Milton? He could do with cheering up.'

Sad Man
Second in the series of the
John Gammon Peak District Crime Thrillers

'Not my type, John.'

'So what is your type, Sandra?'

Sandra paused for a moment and thought should she be brave or would he take offence... she chose not to be totally honest but to give John an indication that she was interested. 'I like a guy to be tall, dark, dress well - I like designer clothes - he needs to make me laugh and be a bit flash.'

John still didn't take the bait. 'That's some guy you are looking for, Sandra.'

Sandra wanted to say that's you but she bottled it. 'Should always aim high, John.'

'Agree, Sandra, now what are you having?'

'I'll have another Rosé please.'

'Coming up.' Sandra went to the ladies while John got the drinks.

Stood at the bar was Pete Barrington, 'Seen much of Joni, then?' The inference was why were you with another woman!

'Just popped in for a quick one straight from work.' Pete never answered. John took the drinks back to the table.

'Who is that guy, John?'

Sad Man
Second in the series of the
John Gammon Peak District Crime Thrillers

'His name is Pete Barrington - think he is a bit annoyed at me - he thinks me and you are an item.'
'Why would that bother him?'

'I am seeing Joni Horalek, and she is a friend of his from Toad Holes.'

'Are you and Joni serious John?'

'No, well, not on my part anyway.' Sandra couldn't help showing her delight that she knew and John had noticed. The night seemed to fly by. 'Are you going to be ok to drive, Sandra?'

This was Sandra's one chance, 'I don't know, John, I feel a bit wobbly.'

'You can stay at mine; I have a spare bed and it's only a couple of mile away at Hittington-in-the-Dale.'

'Are you sure you don't mind, John?'

'Would not be much of a friend if I let you drive now, would I?'

John and Sandra finished their drinks and John got them back to his cottage. As they approached the kitchen door, the moment was there - John looked at Sandra's big brown eyes sparkling like Tiffany diamonds and her slender figure accentuated in the shadow of the full moon. They kissed for a few

Sad Man
Second in the series of the
John Gammon Peak District Crime Thrillers

moments then both pulled away; Sandra made the excuse that John was seeing somebody and John said it was wrong to mix work and leisure. John was thinking about Vicky and the trouble that had caused. They both apologised and then laughed. 'Come on, Sandra, let's get in and have a coffee.'

'I just need to phone Mum and let her know I am staying with a friend or she will be worried - she has Rosie for me tonight.'

'No problem, how do you like your coffee?'

'Just black, no sugar please, John.' John obliged and they sat talking.

'So you were married then, John?'

'Yes.'

'What happened, if you don't mind me asking?'

'I came up here for the serial killer case and she liked London. Looking back, we were drifting apart - she loved the social scene and I loved my job so I guess it was inevitable.'

'So are you divorced now then?'

'Yeah she is with some pompous toff playboy - they are well suited.'

Sad Man
Second in the series of the
John Gammon Peak District Crime Thrillers

'I always admired you when your brother died like he did - you were so brave but I thought you would go back to London.'

'Thought about it very much but Mum and Dad wanted me to stay and I didn't feel I could go after they lost Adam. Now Dad has died so there is just Mum on her own.'

'Perhaps we should introduce your Mum and my Mum, bet they would have a whale of a time.'

'You might have something there, Sandra.' It was almost 2am when they realised the time. 'Look, really enjoyed your company, Sandra, but we have a heavy day tomorrow.'

'Ok, John, we must do it again.'

'Yes, I would like that.' John showed Sandra to her room. 'There are towels and stuff in the en suite Sandra.'

'Great, goodnight, John.'

John lay in bed thinking. What was he thinking - he was seeing Joni and had not got over Vicky who was now back in the picture plus he worked closely with Sandra. That was John though, the women had always fallen at his feet from when he was sixteen. Lineman used to say if women were rabbits, Gammon would have a Coney coat out of the scalps he pulled over the years. *Always one with a saying, Offside what a boy.* John settled down and was soon fast asleep. The light from the morning sun shone brightly through the summer curtains. John rolled over to look at his alarm clock - it was 7.40am. He climbed in the shower and got changed, went downstairs and there was note from Sandra. 'Thanks for a lovely evening, John, called a taxi to get my car so I could get back and get changed hope I didn't disturb you. Sandra x'

John felt a little relieved that he didn't have to make small talk now they were both sober. He just hoped she would be professional at work. John arrived at Bixton spot on 9am and was met by the Head of The Police Complaints Committee, Terry Raybould. 'Superintendent Gammon, my team have found nothing untoward at your station - the towel that Mr Minolis hung himself with should not have been there but hindsight is something we all wish we had. I will conclude in my report that Mr Minolis would have been in such a state of mind to find some way of killing himself and we as a police force cannot cover every option. Good day to you, Mr Gammon.'

'Good day, Mr Raybould,' and they parted company.

Sad Man
Second in the series of the
John Gammon Peak District Crime Thrillers

Gammon immediately phoned Vicky Wills. 'Good news, Vicky,' and he repeated Mr Rayboulds findings.

'That's good news, John.'

'Are you ok, Vicky?'

'I am on the train on my way back up to Bixton so will see you about lunchtime - can you pick me up at the station, it arrives in at 12.10pm?'

'Yes of course, Vicky.'

The intrigue was getting John concerned; Vicky didn't sound too happy. John grabbed a coffee and met Scooper coming out of the ladies toilet. There was no embarrassing silence, Scooper just said good morning and John replied with his own greetings, then they parted and carried on as normal.

John sat down and decided to wade through his paperwork. Top of the pile was a letter from the Chief Constable at the Met, Sir Andrew Herwin. John read the letter and it was basically offering a post back in the Met in a new unit; the Home office wanted a team set up to tackle European Drug Lords and the influx of European hard drugs. He had a number to call and the letter said to call the number after 6pm at night, which John thought was a bit strange.

Sad Man
Second in the series of the
John Gammon Peak District Crime Thrillers

He neatly folded the letter and put it in his inside coat pocket and moved on to the next letter. Most of the piles were run of the mill stuff but then he found a hand written letter and immediately recognised the handwriting; it was the guy who had sent him a letter to the cottage.

The letter had only a few lines on it and it just said;

'Hope you feel bad about little Mary Wells, John boy, it's down to you that this is still going on because you can't catch me. I think I will treat myself this weekend and kill one again. Have a nice day, Johnny Boy ☺'

John took the letter down to Isobel in Forensics. 'I need you to check this for DNA please. What about the trousers, Isobel, did they come up with anything?'

'Nothing, Sir, they were so clean any DNA had well gone.'

'Damn, he has to slip up at some point.'

'He is certainly clever; the DNA off Mary Wells was inconclusive also.'

John felt a little deflated but he knew he had to be positive. He had complicated his private life and

Sad Man
Second in the series of the
John Gammon Peak District Crime Thrillers

now it looked like a dream job back at the Met might complicate things further. It was soon lunchtime so John set off for Bixton railway station. Vicky's train was on time and she climbed out of First Class with not a hair out of place. John met her and took her overnight bag off her. 'Do you fancy some lunch?'

'Yes ok, John, I need to talk to you. What about Up the Steps Maggie's? I hear they do nice lunches.'

'Can do if you want.' John was hoping Pete Barrington wasn't going to be propping up the bar when John walked in with yet another woman. Cursing his luck, sure enough Pete was at the bar. Vicky sat down while John fetched the drinks. 'Hi, can I have a diet coke and a Britvic 55 with ice please.'

'Change of woman again.'

'Look, what is your problem with me?'

'I don't like to see my friends mucked about.'

'For the last time, the lady last night was a fellow officer and that lady is my boss, ok,' and John stared at Pete.

'Are you eating, Sir?' the young girl behind the bar broke the steely silence.

Sad Man
Second in the series of the
John Gammon Peak District Crime Thrillers

'Oh, yes please.'

'These are the menus and the specials board is over there, somebody will be over to take your order, I have put the drinks on a tab, Sir.'

'Great, thank you.'

'What was that all about at the bar?'

'The guy thinks I am seeing you - he is a friend of Joni's.'

'Shall I kiss you and make him really mad?'

'Well I would like that, Vicky, but I don't think it would help the situation.'

'Ok, I will behave. Let's order first.'

'Hi, my name is Monica and I will be your server today, have you decided?'

'Yes please, I will have the Sweet Onion Goats Cheese Tart with the Rocket Salad and Mango Purée please.'

'And for you, Sir?'

'I'll have Steak and Stilton Pie with Cracked Red Wine Potatoes and the Medley of Vegetables.'

'Ok, it will be about a half an hour, is that ok?'

Sad Man
Second in the series of the
John Gammon Peak District Crime Thrillers

'No problem, thank you.'

'So good news on the Minolis report then, Vicky, I thought you would have been doing cartwheels.'

'I am pleased, John, more for Di Trimble than for myself.'

'Yes, she will be a good officer one day, Vicky.'

'Well to be honest, John, I thought you might have told me about the job offer from the Met.'

'How did you know? I only opened the letter a couple of hours ago!'

'John, you and your post - you always open it late - they sent the offer almost a week ago and they said they had not heard from you and thought you were not interested. That's why I was summoned to London - they really want you to have it. The job is a bit like MI5 - you would be heading up a task force of about thirty officers for the job in hand. I have to say, John, it sounds like a great opportunity in your career.'

'I hear what you say and I would be excited about it but a couple of things; I don't want to let you down with this case and I feel I owe my family - I want to nail Lund. My Mum relies on me now that Dad and Adam are gone. Finally, I have to admit I am not over you, Vicky.'

Sad Man
Second in the series of the
John Gammon Peak District Crime Thrillers

'Well do not stay here for me, what will be, will be, John. You have worked too hard in your career and they are throwing you a lifeline to get it back on track after our episode.'

'I don't know, Vicky.'

'Well I told Lord Stathom you would call him by the weekend.'

'That's two days away, Vicky.'

'I know, John, but if you don't take it they have somebody else lined up although you are their first preference.'

'Ok, I will let them know an answer in a couple of days.'

They finished the meal and John paid the bill. Pete Barrington was still staring at John. They arrived back at Bixton station and John walked down to the incident room. 'What happened to you. Sir?'

'Sorry, Sergeant?'

'The race - I thought you were coming to run, Sir.'

'Oh blimey, Carl, I totally forgot, I am so sorry.'

'No problem, Sir, thought you must have forgotten - you have a lot on your plate.

Sad Man
Second in the series of the
John Gammon Peak District Crime Thrillers

The incident room was full with of all John's staff busily working. 'Ok, listen up everyone. We are not having any joy with the killer so I am open to suggestions; one being we plant a decoy.'

'Oh you mean like dress Evans up, Sir, and plant him in Buxton.'

'Very funny, Smarty arse, just a suggestion, any volunteers?'

Di Trimble stepped forward, 'I will do it, Sir.'

'You do realise the ramifications of this, don't you Trimble?'

'Yes. Sir, that's why I joined the police service.'

'Ok, let's go for this tonight - I want you all available for this. I want Trimble fully wired and contactable at all times. Trimble, if for some reason you lose communication then you abort, is that clear?'

'Yes, Sir.'

This was a gamble on Gammon's part but he had to do something. 'Everyone, meet back at the incident room at 2100 hours, ok, let's get on, its going to be a long day.'

Sad Man
Second in the series of the
John Gammon Peak District Crime Thrillers

Scooper came over to Gammon, 'Are you sure Trimble can handle this? She is a rookie, Sir. I don't mind stepping in.'

'If any of the suspects are actually the killer then they have all seen you but have not possibly seen Di Trimble so we have to hope she can handle it.'

'Your call, Sir.' Gammon filled Vicky in with the evenings plans; she wasn't over the moon about Di Trimble being the bait but understood John had no choice. The day dragged somewhat. John was buzzing at the thought they might catch somebody and he had put the new appointment decision to the back of his mind. Everyone assembled at 7pm in the incident room. Di Trimble had been wired for contact.

'Ok, Di, are you comfortable with this? If not, shout up now.'

'I'm fine, Sir.'

'Ok, everybody, this is the plan; Dave Smarty - I want you in the Spread Eagle; this is where the girls will go. Scooper, I want you and Trimble together the whole time and at some point in the night I want Milton to chat you up and I want you to leave Di on her own. I then want you two to get in the back of the white van parked outside Greggs on Marigold Street - I will be in there directing operations. We

Sad Man
Second in the series of the
John Gammon Peak District Crime Thrillers

chose this street because it is close to where Dana Bryant was attacked and that is where I want you to wander too. Di, act a little drunk if you can, head for Greggs - down the side of Greggs is an alleyway leading to Bridge Street - go down there. Evans and Bannon, I want you outside in radio contact with everyone. Bradbury, I want you seemingly drunk in the Spread Eagle. Leave when Trimble leaves but keep well back - I don't want to spook our target. Once Trimble reaches Greggs, keep well back, and then sit on the bench outside Next. We will take over from there. Ok, everybody, let's do this - good luck.'

Everything was in place. Trimble and Scooper smiled at a couple of guys as they went in the Spread Eagle. The Eagle was a big Victorian pub with a dance floor so everyone congregated where they could have a dance. The girls ordered a drink. It was a good hour before the first chancer came along. 'Hi, girls, my names Dick, do you like it?'

'Not that old line,' Scooper said as if she had heard it before.

'Let me get you two a drink, my real name's Mickey, do you like bacon and eggs?'

DI Trimble was the first to answer, 'I do, why?'

'Well that's all I have got in for our breakfast!'

Sad Man
Second in the series of the
John Gammon Peak District Crime Thrillers

'Go away, you little creep,' and they both turned their backs. Di was laughing, which made Scooper chuckle.

A few minutes later a guy about six foot two tall with jet-black hair started chatting Di up. 'Fancy a dance, gorgeous?'

'No, but I bet my mate does,' and before Sandra knew it she was on the dance floor. The night took pretty much the same pattern until just after Bradbury started dancing with Scooper.

Jim Reynolds came up close, 'You on your own, darling?' Reynolds didn't know Trimble, especially as she was made up for the part she was playing but she was aware of him. Trimble was thinking *what a plonker* but had to go along with it.

'Yeah, looks like my mate's copped off.'

'I saw that guy take her dancing - looks like a lively kitten that one.'

'Do you fancy going somewhere a bit quieter?'

'Can do if you want.'

'There is a great little bar on Bridge Street.'

'Ok, let's go, what's your name?'

'Just call me Mac.'

Sad Man
Second in the series of the
John Gammon Peak District Crime Thrillers

'Where are you from, Mac?'

'Up north, Pet.'

'So what are you doing down here?'

'Hopefully copping off with you. What's your name?'

'Di.'

'Nice to meet you, Di, let's get off.'

Trimble's heart was pumping, *had she snared the killer? What was next?* They went outside; Bradbury and Scooper had clocked her so they radioed Gammon. 'Bloody Jim Reynolds, ok, everyone, get in place.' As Reynolds and Trimble walked down the steps of the Spread Eagle Reynolds touched Trimble inappropriately.

'What are you doing, Mac?'

'Come on, let's have some fun.'

'But I have only just met you and I'm not like that.'

'You weren't until you met me,' and he laughed.

'That's the first time I have heard him laugh and all the victims said the rapist laughed at them We may just have our man here, Smarty.'

'I hope so, Sir.'

Sad Man
Second in the series of the
John Gammon Peak District Crime Thrillers

'Don't let Trimble out of your site - she is in danger, I repeat, she is in danger.' Trimble and Reynolds were now at the side of the van. Reynolds noticed a Newcastle sticker on the back window and he started banging on the van panels about Newcastle not being as good as Sunderland. Gammon wanted to jump out and rip his head off.

Trimble pulled him away, 'I thought we were going to have some fun, Mac?'

'Come on then, pretty girl, I know a shortcut down here to the pub.' Halfway down the alleyway he started kissing and fondling Trimble; she tried to push him off so he hit her with the back of his hand.

Gammon shouted, 'Go, go, go.' Milton was first there and he dropped Reynolds to his knee with one blow of his truncheon.

'I am arresting you for molesting a police officer, attacking a police officer and the rape of Dana Braint,' and he read him is rights.

'Good work, team, throw him in the van and haul his sorry ass down to Bixton Police cells.'

All the officers felt relieved as the police van drove off with Reynolds inside. 'How are you, Di?'

'Good thank you, Sir, probably have a black eye in the morning, though.'

Sad Man
Second in the series of the
John Gammon Peak District Crime Thrillers

'I tell you what, everyone back to the Tow'd Man - they are open until 1am and they have a talent contest and open mike on. First round is on me.' They all arrived back at the Tow'd Man and the pub was packed. 'Evening Denis.'

'Hello, John, have you ever heard such bloody noise? Why do they have to sing so loud? Perry Como never did. What you having lad?'

'Hobgoblin for me, Sandra?'

'Brandy and coke please, Sir.'

'Di?'

'Gin and Tonic please.'

'Evans?'

'Hobgoblin, boss, please.'

'Bradbury?'

'Same for me.'

'Bannon?'

'Same for me, Sir.'

'Smarty?'

Sad Man
Second in the series of the
John Gammon Peak District Crime Thrillers

'Just a coke, I'm driving. Only joking, boss, I'll have a Stella please.'

'Milton?'

'Jack Daniels honey whisky for me please, Sir.'

'Ok, have I got everyone?'

'Cheers everybody, great night's work - special thanks to Di - well done.'

As the night got closer to 1am, most of John's crew had left except Scooper. The guy on the microphone shouted, 'Come on, let's finish off with a slow dance - Lady in Red.'

Scooper grabbed John. 'Are you not going to take your Lady in Red then?'

Five pints of Hobgoblin and double vodka took care of that answer. Scooper seductively entwined herself on Gammon. John started to think that he quite liked this. Scooper was being professional at work so what the hell. The dance finished and John made his excuse to go to the toilet and in the hallway, he met Clara. 'What are you playing at, John? That Joni seemed like a really nice girl - who is this one hanging on your every word?'

'She is a work colleague, Clara, nothing else.'

Sad Man
Second in the series of the
John Gammon Peak District Crime Thrillers

'You make sure it stays that way - never shit on your own doorstep, John.' John smiled and carried on to the toilet.

On returning to the bar there was no one there except Denis. 'You ok, lad, shall I get you a taxi? I can take you home if you want - it's not far and that young lady you were dancing with has already gone in the taxi - she said to tell you she will see you tomorrow.'

'Oh ok, Denis, if you don't mind.'

'Of course not, lad, I'll just get my coat.'

Denis dropped John at his cottage. John was feeling a little bemused by Scooper's actions - *I guess time will tell,* he thought.

John woke to a beautiful morning and the cottage was bathed in sunlight. Butterflies were all over the buddleia plant by the kitchen door. *Another day - now we have a suspect in custody - Jim Reynolds.* This was going to John's first task of the day. Hanney had put Reynolds in interview room one with Evans and Bradbury. They were just waiting on Gammon.

Bradbury said the necessary words for the tape as Gammon came in the room. 'Now then, Jim, it looks like we have you bang to rights here. We have given you a lawyer seeing that you refused

Sad Man
Second in the series of the
John Gammon Peak District Crime Thrillers

one - Mr Barwick will represent you. So, last night, you tried to force yourself on PC Di Trimble in virtually the same place as Dana Braint, why Jim?'

'Looking like she was coming on to me all night. I don't know the area and stumbled across the alleyway. You ain't pinning anything on Jim Reynolds I can tell you that now.'

'The night Dana Braint was raped, you said it was a load of rubbish - we also found out you were in the Spread Eagle that night too and you have no alibi for the night of the rape. Then last night you were in the same pub and you attacked PC Di Trimble for no reason.'

'Rubbish, she was coming on to me, they all do.'

'Who is 'all', Jim, explain that one to me.'

'Well, I'm not bad looking and I keep myself fit and women like that - especially the young ones - but I never touched Dana and I only tried to have a bit of fun with her,' and he pointed to PC Di Trimble.

'Do you like being in charge, Jim? Get a kick from it do you? We know you like to slap women - look at Mrs Braint.'

'We are not together, now.'

'Hardly surprising, Jim, the way you hit her, is it?'

Sad Man
Second in the series of the
John Gammon Peak District Crime Thrillers

'Nothing to do with that, I just lost my temper that once - it's all this bloody hassle you lot keep giving me.'

'Oh I haven't even started yet. Where are you living now, Jim?'

'Pritwich - flat 3, Pump Hill Row.'

'We would like to search your premises, Jim, will you allow this or do we need a search warrant?'

Reynolds's felt in his pocket and threw a set of keys on the table. 'It's the one that say's number 3 on it,' and he smiled.

'Thank you, Jim. Ok, end this session but you will be detained, Mr Reynolds.'

'What for?'

'Assault on a police officer for starters.'

'This is bullshit.'

'Put him back in the holding cells, PC Bradbury.'

As John left the interview room, Sergeant Hanney met him, 'Chief Constable Wills wants you, Sir.'

'Ok,, thanks Sergeant.' Gammon grabbed a coffee from the vending machine; he was never sure why he drank it as at best it resembled coloured dishwater. Gammon knocked on Wills door.

'Come in.

'Oh hi John, come in, we have had some information on the Tink lad. Apparently he was seen with two big guys out near Cowdale about two hours ago so he is still about.'

'Right, Ma'am, I'll get some of the team out and about looking for him. Did they get a registration for the car?'

'Apparently not, but it was a light blue Volvo estate.' Just as Vicky finished her sentence, Hanney came to the door.

'We have just taken a call from a farmer in Cowdale - he has found a young lad in one of his barns that he stores hay in. The kid had hung himself. The farmer said he cut him down and tried tom revive him but he was dead.'

'Thanks, Sergeant, arrange for Scooper to get out there with an ambulance and the forensic team please.'

'Yes, Sir.'

'Shit, Vicky, this doesn't sound good.'

Sad Man
Second in the series of the
John Gammon Peak District Crime Thrillers

'Are you thinking what I'm thinking - the Tink boy?'

'Yes I am and I think Lund and his henchmen have something to do with it. I am going to get over there.'

When Gammon arrived, he wasn't expecting to see what he did - the whole barn was ablaze. Scooper had called the fire service. This heightened Gammon's suspicions that this wasn't suicide; they wanted to clear the evidence with a fire. Scooper wandered over to Gammon. 'Not good, Sir, it was ablaze when we got here. There is also a car that's been set alight further down the road - whoever did this knew how to cover their tracks.'

'When the fire is out I want forensics to crawl all over the barn and the car down the road - cordon off all round this field and the vehicle please, Scooper.'

'Yes, Sir.' Gammon was struggling with Scooper's apparent coldness towards him but he had to concentrate on the matter in hand first. Walking back to the car his phone rang it was his Mum.

'Hi, John, could you pop round to see me tonight? I want to discuss something with you.'

'Yeah of course, Mum, are you ok?'

Sad Man
Second in the series of the
John Gammon Peak District Crime Thrillers

Yes fine, son, I will speak to you later. Bye for now,' and she hung up. *More intrigue to deal with,* John thought.

Gammon called Vicky to explain the situation. 'Did the lady that saw Tink in the car get a look at the two guys, Ma'am?'

'She says not - she said she only recognised Tink because of the poster in the Micklock Mercury last week.'

'Think I will take Scooper to see Lund again and see what I can squirm out of the scumbag.'

'Ok, John, keep me up to speed.'

'Will do, Ma'am.'

'Scooper, come with me.'

'Where are we going, Sir?'

'Derby. I think Brian Lund has something to do with this.' As they left Cowdale, Gammon asked Scooper if she was ok.

'Fine, Sir, why?'

'Nothing, only you left in a hurry last night.'

'I decided it's best to keep work and social separate, Sir'.

Sad Man
Second in the series of the
John Gammon Peak District Crime Thrillers

'Ok, Sandra, fine by me,' although he did feel a little miffed that she had blown him out.

'What are you thinking about Lund, Sir?'

'Well Tink disappeared from the pub he frequents and he runs his operations from there. Tink was seen with two guys in a light blue Volvo and I was told a few minutes ago that one of Lund's henchmen had reported his light blue Volvo missing early this morning.'

'What a bloody coincidence - see what you are saying, Sir.' They arrived on the outskirts of Derby at a village called Arkwright. Lund's house stood out; it was on a hill overlooking the village - a new build and must have been worth in the region of £4 million. 'Wow, Sir, is this all from the rackets he runs?'

'We believe so, but he is slippery we can't nail anything on him.'

They arrived at the large green gates and Gammon pressed the Intercom. 'Mr Lund's residence?'

'My name is Superintendent John Gammon and I would like a word with Mr Brain Lund.'

'Just a moment, Sir, I'll see if Mr Lund will accept you.' And the Intercom went dead.

Sad Man
Second in the series of the
John Gammon Peak District Crime Thrillers

'Bloody accept me? Cheeky bastard.'

'It's ok, Sir, the gates are opening.' They drove about a quarter of a mile up the drive arriving at the palatial mansion where Gammon and Scooper were met by the butler.

'Mr Lund will see you in the drawing room, Mr Gammon,' and he showed them into a room with a grand piano and oil paintings hanging on the wall; this oozed money. Lund spoilt the ambience by walking in with a big Cuban cigar wearing a purple and yellow shell suit. On his arm was a very pretty girl in her mid twenties - she had long dark hair and was dressed to kill, dripping in diamonds.

'Well if it ain't my old adversary, Johnny Boy Gammon, and what's your name, pretty lady?'

Scooper never replied. 'Mr Lund, would it be possible to ask you a few questions?'

'Without my lawyer?'

'If possible, Mr Lund.'

'Well, just for you, Johnny Boy, because I feel sorry for you,' and he laughed. Lund told the arm candy to leave. 'Right, now how can I help you?'

'Mark Anthony Tink ring any bells, Mr Lund?'

Sad Man
Second in the series of the
John Gammon Peak District Crime Thrillers

'Sorry, no.'

'Just so you are aware - Mark Anthony Tink was at a pub where you and your closest friends frequent and he was being watched by us. Tink had a big guy come up to him and say something in his ear they then both left the bar and went in the back room. He was never seen again. We believe - although this hasn't yet been confirmed - that he was found hung in Cowdale today but when the police arrived the barn was on fire as was a Light blue Volvo car just down the road.'

Lund looked at Gammon in his smug arrogant way, puffed on his cigar then said. 'How do you want me to help you, Johnny Boy?'

Gammon despised Lund but was trying to be professional. 'Let's start by saying where were you from the time of last night leading up to this afternoon and the discovery of the body by the farmer?'

'Now let me just think about this, Johnny Boy. Oh yes, I was here at home.'

'Can anyone vouch for you, Mr Lund?'

'Lola, my girlfriend, who you just met. My butler, Eric Falstaff, and some of my friends - we had a game of Poker until 4am. I won of course.'

Sad Man
Second in the series of the
John Gammon Peak District Crime Thrillers

'Of course,' said John - he just could not help himself.

'Do I detect a little jealousy there, Johnny Boy?'

'Not in the least, Mr Lund, do any of your friends that you had invited over have a light blue Volvo car?'

'If you had checked your records, Johnny Boy, you would know that the vehicle was stolen from here sometime this morning - the owner, Jimmy the Iron, stayed the night here.'

'How can a car get pinched from this property with all the security you have and the electric gates?'

'I know, Mr Gammon, it's amazing what these criminal people can do can do these days. I hear if you cut a tennis ball in half and place it over a lock on a car door then strike the tennis ball it opens the central locking system. I really must get my security looked at, Johnny Boy. Now have you got any more questions? Only it's time for my massage.'

'Ok, Mr Lund, I am sure we will meet again.'

'I will look forward to it, give my regards to your mother.' Scooper held Gammon back as Gammon pointed his finger at Lund.

Sad Man
Second in the series of the
John Gammon Peak District Crime Thrillers

'One day, Lund, you will live to regret this.'

'Mr Falstaff, show Mr Gammon and his bird out please.'

'With pleasure, Sir.'

Gammon and Scooper got back in the car and set off back to Bixton. 'What an obnoxious twerp, Sir.'

'I could say something stronger but won't, Sandra.' When they arrived back at Bixton, Vicky called John to the office.

'They managed to salvage some teeth from the body, John. I am afraid he is almost not unrecognisable but it is Mark Anthony Tink.'

'I better go and see his parents, Vicky, this is the worst part of the job.'

'I know, John, it's never easy.'

'Trouble is, I feel we have some blame here - we wired him up and once they found that, his life was over.'

'Nothing we can do, John, he was mixed up with these scumbags way before we wired him.'

'I know, Vicky, but it doesn't stop me feeling bad about it. Right, well I will get over and inform his parents then I am calling it a night; my Mum wants to speak with me.'

'That sounds ominous, John.'

'We will see, Vick, see you tomorrow. Try and hang onto Reynolds for as long as you can - I am trying to get under his skin to try and make him talk.'

'Will do, John, speak tomorrow - good luck.'

'Thanks, Vicky,' and John left.

John drove to The Cherries, Gullet Lane in Swinster. This was not going to be easy. As he approached the front door, Mr Tink opened it. 'Have you got news, Mr Gammon?'

'Can I come in please?'

'Certainly.'

Mrs Tink came from the kitchen, 'Have you found him?'

'Please would you sit down.' Mr and Mrs Tink sat on the settee and John sat in the chair. 'I am very sorry to say, we found your son today and I am afraid he is dead.'

Mrs Tink flew into an uncontrollable rage, 'You have caused this - my poor boy!' Mr Tink restrained her.

Sad Man
Second in the series of the
John Gammon Peak District Crime Thrillers

'Where is he, Mr Gammon, can we see him?'

'Sir, I feel it could be too distressing for you and your wife - he is very badly burnt.'

Mr Tink was now crying, 'What happened?'

'We had a report today that your boy was seen in a light blue Volvo with two men and within two hours of this sighting a farmer found your boy in his barn hanging in what looked like a suicide.'

'What do you mean - looked like a suicide?'

'By the time my officers got on the scene, the barn had been set alight and the car was also found further down the road ablaze.'

'You think he was murdered?'

'It's early days, Mr Tink, but that is a line of investigation we are pursuing. Would you like me to call a relative or a friend? We have trained grief councillors I can arrange to come over.'

'No, we will be fine, Mr Gammon, thank you.'

'Then I will leave you to grieve and I am very sorry for your loss. I will be in touch, Mr Tink.' John left the family in shreds. He was thinking how dreadful it must have been for them. He then thought to

Sad Man
Second in the series of the
John Gammon Peak District Crime Thrillers

Lund giving it large like nothing mattered, *he had to be involved.*

John's mind was everywhere - should he phone Joni or not? He felt he betrayed her and he also felt this relationship meant more to Joni than ultimately it did to him. Although he knew it wasn't right not to phone he could not face falling out so he decided to leave it. His mind wasn't in the best state after just telling a couple that their son had died.

Driving up through Swinster, John noticed Bob's car in the car park. This was the only excuse John needed so he swung into the car park promising himself he would just have a couple then leave.

'A pint of Pedigree please, Kev.'

'Coming up, John, rum do about that young lad - they are saying he was murdered.'

'We don't know yet, Kev, he was badly burnt but nothing is being ruled out at the moment.'

'You better get Bob and Cheryl one.'

'What are you two having?'

'Thanks, John, I'll have a Stella please, Kev.'

'And for madam?'

Sad Man
Second in the series of the
John Gammon Peak District Crime Thrillers

'A vodka and tonic please, thanks, John.'

'No Joni tonight?'

'Just left work, Cheryl, been a heavy day today so decided to call for a quick one and have an early night.'

'I saw your Mum and your Uncle Graham in town earlier. You are his spitting image John.'

'Yes, a lot of people say that.'

'If I didn't know your Mum better, I would say you were his lad,' and she laughed!

John's thoughts returned to the day his Mum told him the man he thought was his father actually wasn't and Uncle Graham was. Funnily enough, Lindsay had once said that he looked nothing like Phil and his looks and his ambition was more like his Uncle Graham.

'John?'

'Sorry, Kev, I was miles away then.'

'Sure, you have a lot on your plate, lad, that will be £9.44 please. Thank you very much, are you lot coming to tho pre-carnival party here Saturday night? It's only £6.00 a head and there is a comedian and a singer on and a buffet about 9.30pm.

'Sorry, Bob, see you and Cheryl have already got yours.'

'Yes, Kev, Doreen sold them to us - I told her if the comedian is no good I would step in.' Cheryl gave him a dig in the ribs.

'That's not happening, Robert.' Kev and John both gave a cheeky smile. Bob being Bob just laughed.

'Are we sitting down? Carol Lestar, Tony and Rita Sherriff are in the snug.'

'Ok, let's do it.'

As soon as Carol saw John she made a beeline for him. 'Come and give your Aunty Carol a hug, my little favourite copper.' As usual John felt embarrassed but played along.

'How's the case going about that young lad they found? He was burned to death in that barn. Nasty business that, and fancy it being on Peter Tupper's land.'

John nearly choked on his beer. 'That wasn't Tuppers land, Tony.'

Sad Man
Second in the series of the
John Gammon Peak District Crime Thrillers

'Oh yes it was, John, they called it Turpin barn because they reckoned Dick Turpin used to hide there after his Highway robberies. I know that's rubbish but it is legend round here.'

'Yes I know that, Tony, but that used to be Harold Drake's place when I was growing up round here.'

'You are correct, John, but when Harold died seven year back, Tupper bought it at auction.'

John's head was reeling - he now had a slight connection to Lund. 'Excuse me a minute, everyone, I need to make a quick call.' John spoke with Scooper. 'I have just been told that the barn where Tink was owned by Peter Tupper - how the hell did we miss this?'

'Sir, the guy that reported finding the boy hung said it was his barn.'

'Bring him back in for questioning. While you are at it, I want all Mark Anthony Tink's mobile phone records looking at and banking records on my desk in the morning. I will see you in the morning.'

'Sir, Evans has already looked at them.'

'Sandra, just do as I have requested, I am going to look through the records.' Scooper was taken aback by John's words.

Sad Man
Second in the series of the
John Gammon Peak District Crime Thrillers

John went back, finished his beer and said his goodbyes. Driving home, John could feel the jigsaw starting to fit together. When he got in there was a message from his Mum - could he call tomorrow night as Uncle Graham wants to have a word. John felt out of his depth on this situation. He understood that his Uncle Graham had been a good brother to Phil but other than that one incident which he was sure he regretted. John didn't want some speech from his Uncle Graham; he had told his Mum he accepted what had happened but as far as he was concerned, Phil was his Dad. He put the receiver down and thought he would call his Mum in the morning. His bed was calling and he had a long day ahead.

As usual, the night seemed short and John was soon back on the road to Bixton. He arrived at the station and could sense the solemn mood. Evans met John. 'Sir, I am afraid we have another victim. We are pretty sure her name is Sharon Bailey; she was reported missing by her parents at 4.00am this morning.'

'Right, get everyone in the incident room. Sergeant Hanney, grab me a coffee please and bring it through.'

'Ok, Sir.'

Sad Man
Second in the series of the
John Gammon Peak District Crime Thrillers

The incident room was silent when Gammon went in. 'Before we start, everyone, I realise the efforts everybody is making on the current two cases but we are being sloppy and it has to stop now.' Everyone hung their heads down. 'Ok, new victim, Sharon Bailey?'

'Just had it confirmed, Sir. She was twenty-three years old and she was on a hen night in Bixton last night. The reason the parents called is one of the girls, a Judy Lowry, called them at 4.00am to say that Sharon didn't get on the bus and they had somehow got split up. Sharon had said she wanted a kebab but the other girls didn't so she went off for one. They had spent almost two hours looking for her and the bus driver said he couldn't wait any longer so they assumed she had got a lift home. Her parents panicked and phoned us. We had patrol cars in Bixton looking for her. At 5.30am this morning a guy on his way into work found a red handbag and as he walked a bit further, he found the body.'

'Right, I want this guy bringing for interview. Scooper, I need you in on this. Trimble, Evans and Smarty - I want you to bring the farmer in who initially found the body of Mark Anthony Tink. The rest of you, I want Mark Anthony Tink's parents' bank accounts studied for any regular cash amounts going in.'

Sad Man
Second in the series of the
John Gammon Peak District Crime Thrillers

'What about Brian Lund, Sir? Shall we take a look at his as well?'

'There would be no point, Sergeant Milton, he is too clever for that. Ok, everyone, get on with it.'

Gammon called at Wills's office before going to look at Mark Anthony's mobile and bank records. 'Hi Vicky, just a quick update.' Vicky looked at Gammon thinking he was about to announce he would be leaving but it wasn't that. 'You ok, Vicky?'

'Yes, John, carry on.'

'There was another victim last night - a Sharon Bailey - we are bringing the guy in who found the body. We are also bringing in the farmer who reported Tink's body. Apparently, that barn belonged to Peter Tupper so there is a Brian Lund connection here I think. We are also going over bank records and mobile records again to see if we have missed anything.'

'Ok, John, I am starting to get some grief from the press and the powers that be - I realise you are all doing your best but I just need something to feed to the circling wolves.'

'Understand, Vicky, I'll let you know.'

'Oh, we have had to let Reynolds go - just had his lawyer on, we had nothing we could really stick on him. We could not really press the charge of assaulting a police officer because on the video in the pub Di was being quite suggestive - it just would not stick.'

'Damn. Ok, Vicky, we will keep trying.'

Gammon went back to his office picking up a coffee on the way. Gammon called down to Hanney. 'Sergeant, ensure before all the interviews finish that I am made aware. I want to speak with the farmer and the guy who found Sharon Bailey's body this morning.'

'Will do, Sir.' Gammon sipped his coffee and started on the Tink records. Almost an hour had passed and Gammon had been over the eighteen sheets of mobile numbers with no luck, then he took a different view and started to look for numbers that were very infrequent and bingo! He called the number and it went to voice mail.

'Johnny the Iron here, don't f*#k with me, just leave a message.' *Brilliant,* Gammon thought, *now we have a common bond.* He made a note of the number and started on the bank records. This was another mammoth task – forty-eight pages to trawl through. Gammon was halfway through when the phone rang.

Sad Man
Second in the series of the
John Gammon Peak District Crime Thrillers

'Mr Vaughan, the farmer, from Cowdale is here, Sir.'

'Ok, I will pop down, Sergeant.' Mr Vaughan was in interview room one with Trimble, Evans and Smarty. The team were a little surprised to see Gammon come in as well.

'Ok, Mr Vaughan, thanks for coming in this morning.' Vaughan was swarthy character, a guy who probably only shaved a couple of times a week; he had a checked shirt - typical famer-type attire with a pair of blue work trousers and an old cream coloured coat which was held together with baler twine.

Vaughan nodded at Gammon. 'Can you run through exactly why you were at this barn?'

'Well, Peter Tupper's land and mine border each other and that barn is actually owned by Peter Tupper but because of some problems with his will since he died there has been nobody looking after it. So I guess I am in trouble but I put some sheep on it - seems a shame to waste good land.'

'Ok, so run through why you went in the barn.'

'Well, about a week ago, I saw a car there.'

'What colour was it, Mr Vaughan?'

Sad Man
Second in the series of the
John Gammon Peak District Crime Thrillers

'I could not tell - it was too dark. I had gone to check on my sheep about two fields away. Anyway, the following day I noticed there had been a padlock put on the barn so I thought I better get my sheep off Mr Tupper's land as it looks like things must have been sorted with his estate and I didn't want to get into any trouble.

'So the other day, I had some time so I went down with my sheepdog, Bessieco, and while she was rounding my sheep up - she was national champion you know...'

'Oh good, Mr Vaughan, but tell us more about the barn.'

'Well, I noticed the lock had been smashed off and it was on the floor. Thinking that people might think I had done it, I thought I best look inside and that's when I found that boy. I had to get my sheep moved but as soon as I did that I came straight here.'

'Did you see anyone hanging about? Why didn't you call us from your mobile?'

'I don't have one of things to stick to my ear - can't be doing with all that at my age. Didn't see anybody when I found the boy the other day. Oh, I just remembered, there were some cardboard boxes stacked in the corner but whoever set light to the barn must have taken them or they were burnt in the fire.'

'Ok, Mr Vaughan, thank you for your time we will be in touch.

'Smarty, have we got the fire department report yet or anything from Forensics?'

'Not yet, Sir.'

'Get onto them please.'

'Will do, Sir.'

'Gut feeling here is - they were storing something in that barn. I also think Lund is involved, most definitely. Evans, see if forensics have got anything at all that we can work with.'

'Will do, Sir.'

Gammon headed for the other interview room to speak to the guy who found Sharon Bailey's body. Scooper pressed the tape and announced the arrival of Gammon.

'Mr...?'

'Bob Bridges, Sir.'

'Hello, Bob, this is just an informal chat but we like to record things as much for your comfort as ours.'

Sad Man
Second in the series of the
John Gammon Peak District Crime Thrillers

'I understand.'

'Do you mind if I call you Bob?'

'Please, go ahead.'

'Ok, Bob, so you were on your way to work - where is that exactly?'

'I work at Stonehead Quarry and I live in Micklock. I love walking so when it's a nice day I set off early and walk to work.'

'What time do you leave your home?'

'I left about 4.20am.'

'You reported the body of the girl at what time exactly?'

'I think from memory it was 5.25am.'

'You seem very sure Bob.'

'I time myself, and the place where I found the girl on the Moor usually takes me about one hour five minutes.'

'So you say you time yourself to this point - what's so special about this point on the Moor, Bob?'

'All the locals call the ditch Alison's drop.'

Sad Man
Second in the series of the
John Gammon Peak District Crime Thrillers

'Do you know why, Bob?'

'Well. legend has it that Old Mr Alison had an affair with a local girl called Kitty Simmons - there is talk he had been seeing her when she worked in the Hydro at Micklock as a receptionist. Not sure if that is what she would have been called in the old days, anyway, Kitty was found strangled and they reckon it was old man Alison. After strangling her, he threw he body down the banking. Because he was a circuit judge, the police in those days were frightened of him so no charges were ever brought and Kitty's only surviving parent, her mother, could not even afford to travel up for Kitty's funeral. Some kind soul did make her a wooden cross with her name on it as a head stone. She is in St Helen's churchyard in Rowksly.'

'Ok, Bob, so you found the body - what did you do next?'

'Well I felt for her pulse but there wasn't one. I'm a trained First Aider, Mr Gammon. Because of where she was I had no mobile signal so I clambered back up the bank and ran towards the Alison House but well before I got there I got a signal so I phoned Bixton Police Station.'

'Ok, Bob, as you are aware, this is not the first victim to be found on Micklock Moor. Did you see anybody this morning?'

Sad Man
Second in the series of the
John Gammon Peak District Crime Thrillers

'No, I never do. Actually, that's not quite true, I did see somebody a few weeks back rushing off the Moor - he looked flustered as if I had disturbed him. He was a big guy and he had a sweatshirt on - it was blue with a logo of something on it.'

'Did he speak?'

'I said good morning but he just brushed past me.'

'Did you see what the logo said on the sweatshirt?' Was it a company logo or a football team or something?'

'Come to think about it, could have been Micklock Town - they have centurion and a lion on their logo - I know because I used to watch them a lot a few years back.'

'Ok, Bob, thanks for your cooperation, we will be in touch during the course of our enquiries.'

'Can I go now, Mr Gammon?'

'Yes, but we will have to corroborate your story with your employer.'

'No problem, Mr Gammon, I hope you find this bastard.'

'Me too, Bob.

Sad Man
Second in the series of the
John Gammon Peak District Crime Thrillers

'Ok, Scooper, let's go up to Stonehead Quarry and see if our Bob is all he says he is.' Scooper and Gammon set off for Stonehead Quarry.

'Stonehead Quarry had been a big employer years back with over three hundred men working there. The Peak Park had cut back their quarrying licence then they had all the trouble with the tree people for about three years protecting the land that the quarry needed to quarry to be viable. In the end, the guys were being laid off all the time so most left and got other jobs; the dozen or so left just really supply local builders or DIY guys.'

'How come you know all this, Scooper?'

'My Mum's cousin worked there for about 27 years until he passed away in May last year. He was Stonehead Quarry through and through.' They pulled into the Quarry and headed for reception, if you could call it that - it was a breezeblock shed basically. There was a woman in her mid fifties at a desk and guy in his seventies sat rocking on his chair.

'How can I help you two lovely people?' said the man.

Gammon and Scooper showed their warrant cards, 'We have a few questions about Mr Bob Bridges.'

Sad Man
Second in the series of the
John Gammon Peak District Crime Thrillers

'Come in, lad, grab a chair, wut tha like a coffee?' He then threw out a hand the size of a shovel for Gammon to shake.

'No, we are both fine thanks, Mr...?'

'Billy Smith my name, dos no lad tha looks just like an ode mate mine - Graham Campbell, I heard he had done good for his sen. He could bloody pull the girlies.'

'His is my uncle, Sir.'

'See I knew tha was a resemblance, so art thou Phil Gammons lad then?'

'Yes I am, Sir.'

'Sorry to hear he had passed away, is thee Mum ok?'

'Could I just ask these questions, Billy? Then we can be out of your hair.' Billy pulled his dusty cap off to reveal no hair at all.

'Tha will have a problem with that ode lad.'

'Does a Mr Bob Bridges work here?'

'He does, lad, never missed a day's work in thirty years but he were late today - said he had found a lass's body at Alison's Drop.'

Sad Man
Second in the series of the
John Gammon Peak District Crime Thrillers

'How did he seem when he came to work, Billy?'

'He were a bit shook up but was ok - that's Bob, he has had a lot of anguish in his life. He is a scout leader and a minibus he was driving went off the road near that Alison mansion; some bloody dog ran out from the Alison House and he swerved but the minibus hit a lorry coming other way. By rights, lorry driver should not have been there - he was takin' a shortcut. All nine scouts were killed but Bob survived and he never got over it. That was almost five year back - he is a nice man Mr Gammon.'

'Ok, Billy, thanks for your time.'

'Hey anytime, Mr G,' and he smiled showing one tooth in the top jaw and one tooth in the bottom jaw.

Once outside, Scooper said, 'Sorry, Sir, but he made me laugh - what a throwback to Derbyshire people of yesteryear! He has a strong accent, hey.'

'Yeah, Scooper, he took some understanding at times. Not sure about Bob though. You know if you think about it - the story of disturbing somebody could be that he was disturbed and that's why he called the police.'

'Any DNA found at the scene?'

Sad Man
Second in the series of the
John Gammon Peak District Crime Thrillers

'Well the doctors are saying that there was sexual intercourse; there was bruising round her upper thighs and she was strangled, but again no DNA. Damn it, Sandra, when are we ever going to get a break?'

'Well I have one this weekend - off to the seaside, Sir.'

'Where Sandra?'

'Whitby. Mum loves fish and chips from that one - they always queue at in the town, think it's called The Magpie.'

'Blimey, that brings back memories - I remember queuing there when we were kids, it was my Dad's favourite place.

'Let's get back to Bixton and call a meeting in the incident room for 4pm please, Sandra.' Gammon had decided he wasn't going to take the job so had to make the call when he got back. Gammon sat pondering in his office. Gammon's office was not the most pleasant place to spend time in.

While he sat pondering he was looking round his office he noticed that it had not been decorated for possibly twenty years with all the outs that had gone on under successive governments. The paper was a dingy-looking colour - whoever had the office prior to John must have been heavy smokers

Sad Man
Second in the series of the
John Gammon Peak District Crime Thrillers

with all the discolouration on the walls. The small window would not open, although, even if it had the only view was of the car park. The carpet was threadbare. What a contrast to his plush office in the Met. John had a large office with leather settees and an oak desk. There was a flat screen TV, which also doubled up as a computer monitor if he wanted to do Powerpoint presentations to his officers. Now he had to be sure that by not taking the job for the Home Office was he finally putting the last nail in his coffin for his career and would Bixton be enough for his talents?

Decision made, John rang the number on the letter - it was immediately answered by Lord Stathon's PA. 'Lord Stathon's office, Maria Arroyo speaking.'

John explained about the letter. Maria stated the letter did say to call after 6pm then John explained because of workload he had not been able to contact the office and time had gone on so he thought he better call now.

'Ok, I will see if Lord Stathon is free.'

John was held on the line for what seemed like an eternity but eventually a very well spoken man answered. 'Mr Gammon, Lord Stathon here - I thought you were never going to contact us.'

Sad Man
Second in the series of the
John Gammon Peak District Crime Thrillers

'Sorry about that, your lordship, things are a little hectic up here.'

'So I am led to believe. I was speaking with your Chief Constable last week. Well, let me outline what we would like you to do, Gammon.' Before John could get a word in, his lordship had outlined the job. The salary was almost twice his current salary. The job did sound very exciting; his only boss would be his lordship who, to be honest, would not have a clue so he would pretty much be his own man.

John Gammon had always been a man of his word and he had told his Mum he was staying so he could not go back on his word. After almost five minutes of non-stop talking, John told his lordship that the job wasn't for him. Stathon was speechless. After a few seconds of eerie silence, Stathon just said, 'Big mistake, young man,' and put the phone down. *Well that's that, then,* thought John, *I can concentrate on the job in hand.*

John's phone rang; 'Have you got a minute, John?'

'I will be through in one second.'

John knocked on Vicky's door. Vicky was sat in a grey business suit - she was otunning. What happened next surprised even John.

Sad Man
Second in the series of the
John Gammon Peak District Crime Thrillers

'I want you to understand, John, you have made a massive mistake - you have made an enemy of Stathon and, trust me, that was not wise. What are you thinking of?'

'With due respect, Vicky, the job was very appealing but I have commitments up here.'

'So you are now going to vegetate in Derbyshire with all your talent? You must be barmy, John.'

'Look, Vicky, my career has always taken first place in my life and it ruined my marriage, killed my brother and I'm pretty sure it killed my father too so I owe my mother something.'

'Ok, John, let's drop the subject - just be aware of what you have done.'

'I hear you. I have called a meeting for 4pm - it's nearly that now, so let's go down to the incident room.'

Everyone had gathered and Gammon could see on the faces of his officers they felt drained. Every little clue they were getting but they could get nothing to stick.

'Afternoon, everyone.' John went over to the incident board. 'Let's see if we are missing something shall we.

Sad Man
Second in the series of the
John Gammon Peak District Crime Thrillers

'Victim number one; Dana Bryant. Dana was raped; she had a connection - one of the suspects, Jim Reynolds, was living with her mother at the time of the incident. Victim number two; Milan Peterson, was raped. Victim number three; Suzy Warner; sadly this girl was raped and murdered - his first murder. Connections with Mark Anthony Tink and Brian Lund; this line of enquiry I feel may lead us to the killer. Fourth victim; Lara Bennett was raped - no obvious connections to any of our suspects, just wrong place, wrong time. Victim number five; Mary Dunham - she escaped her attacker. Was the attacker disturbed or was this some kind of copycat case? Victim number six; Jane Wells was raped, and by the doctors report, quite violently. Victim number seven; Sharon Bailey - another rape and this girl he also murdered. That's five rapes and two rapes with murder. A gentleman called Bob Bridges found Sharon on his way to work. Again, did he find her or was he the attacker and also disturbed another strong line of enquiry? I believe Sharon was found here at a local named landmark, Alison' drop. Funny how we keep coming back to the Alison's, hey?

'Right, any questions anyone? PC Trimble?'

'Sir, looking at the incident board; a couple of things are jumping out at me. We all know Eric Stein was tried for rape - he is the gardener at the Alison

Sad Man
Second in the series of the
John Gammon Peak District Crime Thrillers

house. When we raided his home, we found articles about the cases in his shed. He has tried to offset this by saying he was only following the cases because he was wrongly accused. He also in my opinion tried to put us off any scent by saying he had heard Miss Alison talking to somebody. Now either Miss Alison has somebody in the house, which we found nothing on the search other than a picture of Miss Alison with a child; or he is covering his tracks. I think we should step up surveillance on Stein, I really think he has something to do with this, Sir. That's all, thank you.'

'Thanks for that, Trimble, anyone else? Yes, Smarty?'

'Reynolds fits the bill for me. We have caught him bang to rights the other night - the guy in my opinion is a serial scumbag. He hits women, he forces himself on women and he was in the Bixton area on two occasions on the same night as Dana Bryant and Suzy Warner were seen and later attacked.'

'I take on board both your input. With this in mind, PC Bannon, I want you in plain clothes shadowing Lund and his buddies. Evans and Bradbury, stake out the Alison house - ensure you are well back though. Milton, shadow Eric Stein next week and, Milton, let's see what we can dig out on Bob Bridges. Inspector Smarty, let's keep a close eye on Lund's house - please check all number plates of any comings and goings. Anyone got any questions?'

'Sir, have you find anything on Mr Tink's bank details yet?'

'No Sandra, if you wish, you can look at these for me. Ok, everyone, chin's up, let's try and get something for next week please.'

'Feel some positives coming through there, John, your team still seem up for the task and that is credit to you.'

'Thanks, Ma'am.'

'John, I just want to say I am sorry for biting your head off earlier but you are a good copper and it seems a waste of your talent out here in the back woods of Derbyshire. I just know how the system works - bloody Lord Stathon and people - it's a bloody secret society in the Home Office and he will make sure your name is blackened because he can't have what he wants.'

'That's as maybe, Ma'am, but I have to think of my Mum - I am all she has now so I feel comfortable I am doing the right thing.'

Sad Man
Second in the series of the
John Gammon Peak District Crime Thrillers

'As I said, I'm sorry, I respect your decision, John. Do you fancy taking me for a quick beer? I have had a nightmare of a day?'

'Yes, of course, fancy some nice food at the Spinning Jenny?'

'Sounds good to me.'

Just then John's phone rang. 'Excuse me, Vicky, I need to take this.'

It was Joni. 'Hi, John, thought I would give you a quick call - have you fallen out with me?'

'Sorry, Joni, work is taking up my time.'

'I understand, John, I don't have to work Saturday or Sunday – if you're free then?'

'Yes, of course, come up to mine Friday night.'

'Ok, better go, Rick is glaring at me and customers are waiting, see you Friday,' and she hung up.

'Was that your little friend, John? Sounds like she is missing you - do you think this meal is a good idea?'

'Of course, Vicky, we are work colleagues.' They both smiled because they both knew different.

Sad Man
Second in the series of the
John Gammon Peak District Crime Thrillers

It was a lovely evening as they both left Bixton. John was in his beloved Jaguar and Vicky in her Mercedes Convertible.   The sun was shining bright.   Climbing out of Bixton, the little row of cottages always had a fantastic show of hanging baskets of every colour - it had become a Bixton tourist attraction although to be fair the cottages were actually in Little Driggin. Nobody really cared though, it had brought the tourists to the little village which now supported a thriving pub, corner shop and chip shop - all of which would most probably have shut if hadn't been for the flower blooms at the cottages.

They finally pulled up at the Spinning Jenny and walked through the oak door to be met by a smiling Kev in his obligatory red dickie bow; it never failed to make John smile. 'Good evening, Sir, Madam, what can I serve you with tonight?'

'And very nice to see you, Kev, what's with the pomp?'

'Oh I am trying out my landlord's skills - I am in the final of the Derbyshire Landlord and Landladies Victuallers Society - you get voted by the public and by secret shoppers at your pubs and if you are pleasant and you are presentable, etc, then you could end up in the final with three other landlords or landladies.'

Sad Man
Second in the series of the
John Gammon Peak District Crime Thrillers

'So how does anyone win?'

'It's black tie evening at Bixton Opera House and you have to do a minimum three minute speech then the audience ask you questions and mark you accordingly. The winner gets a holiday for two, all expenses paid plus spending money and this time it's a cruise around the Caribbean islands. You also get a plaque that you can show in your pub. Anyway, I entered it five year ago but didn't get to the final so I am going to make sure I am on the ball this time.'

'Wished I'd not asked, Kev, wait until I tell Steve.'

'Don't tell him, he gives me enough stick now, John,' and he laughed. 'Right, what would you like?'

'Could I have a French Martini please?'

'You certainly can, Madam, and for you bugger lugs.'

'That's no way to practise, Kev,' and John laughed. 'I'll have a pint of Pedigree. Have you got a table for two Kev?'

'Here's the gaffer - she'll tell you.'

'Hello, John, lovely to see you - and who is this?'

Sad Man
Second in the series of the
John Gammon Peak District Crime Thrillers

'You better behave, this is my boss from work, Vicky Wills.'

'Very pleased to meet you, dear. So, table for two is it?'

'Yes, please.'

'Can fit you in but it will half an hour I'm afraid.'

'That's fine, Doreen. Let's sit over here, Vicky.' Ted Baker nodded in approval; he was a man of few words was Ted but he had been drinking in the Spinning Jenny for as long as John could remember.

The Spinning Jenny was unusually quiet in the bar although the restaurant was very busy. 'Well, John, other than work, how are you?'

'To be honest, Vicky, I seem to have so much going on. I will tell you something, but please don't repeat it. We were looking through some old pictures just after Dad died and Mum drops the bombshell that my Dad wasn't my biological father.'

'Oh, John, I am sorry.'

'Funnily enough, it rocked me but not how you would expect.'

'So do you know who your father is?'

Sad Man
Second in the series of the
John Gammon Peak District Crime Thrillers

'Well this is the best bit, it's my Uncle Graham. You see, Vicky, people have always commented that I looked like him; he has dark hair like me and my Dad had blonde, slightly ginger coloured hair. I can't tell you the amount of times people have remarked how much me and my Uncle Graham look alike and how he was very driven just like me.'

'So you say you are coping with it ok, John?'

'I am, Vicky, but my Mum wants me to speak with Uncle Graham and I'm not ready for that. You see, my Dad, or the guy who I thought was my Dad, meant everything to me - a better father nobody could wish for.'

'Did Phil know?'

'He was never told but I truthfully don't know. If he did, he never let on - I truly hope he never did because he will always be my Dad.'

'Ok, you two, your table is ready.'

'Wow, Doreen, you have been busy.' The restaurant had all new carpets, wallpaper and it was really set up more like a top restaurant.

'Our chef, Richie, asked if he could make some alterations - he has done this on his off day, we only had to close the restaurant for one other day.'

Sad Man
Second in the series of the
John Gammon Peak District Crime Thrillers

'Well, it looks amazing, Doreen.'

'Thank you, John, now what can I get you to drink?'

'Do you fancy a Chablis, Vicky?'

'Sound good to me, John.'

'Ok, I will have the Chablis Premier Cruz please, Doreen.'

'Great choice, John, I love this one. I will give you a minute to look at the menu but on special tonight we have Bacon wrapped Toads in a Leek filled Hole, Caramelised Heritage Carrot Risotto, Roast Fillet of Aberdeen Angus Beef with Braised Jacobs Ladder Asparagus, White Cabbage and Baby Roast Potatoes. I will be back in a minute.'

'Wow, John, this looks fantastic, and the prices are so good - any wonder they are doing so well.'

'Guess they have always had a good reputation for food but Richie is taking it to the next level and to be honest, I think it's not like the pressure cooker environment that he had in London.'

Doreen arrived back; Vicky sampled the wine and gave it a big thumbs up. 'So what would you like to eat?'

'Spoilt for choice here, Doreen.'

Sad Man
Second in the series of the
John Gammon Peak District Crime Thrillers

'Can I have the Seared Scallops with Leeks and Lemon Chilli Butter please, Doreen?'

'And I will have Water Cress and Celeriac Soup with Goats Cheese Croutons please, Doreen.'

'Ok now your mains?'

'Just noticed he has got my favourite dish - he used to do this in London so I've got to have that. I will have the stuffed saddle of Lincolnshire Rabbit with Mrs Harrops Black Pudding, Butter Glazed Jersey Potatoes and Roasted Vegetables please, Doreen.'

'He has an advantage here, Doreen,' and Vicky laughed. 'I'll try The Cumbrian Suckling Pig with King Cabbage and Granola Clusters, thank you.'

'Very busy, as you can see, so you may have to wait a little longer than normal.'

'No problem, thanks.'

'So you were saying, Phil didn't know? Hope you don't think I am prying, John.'

'Absolutely not, Vicky, it's helping me sharing this with you because I know I can trust you. Mum is talking of selling up and I have a gut feeling she is thinking of moving closer to Uncle Graham – I think she knows Derbyshire is not enough for me forever.'

Sad Man
Second in the series of the
John Gammon Peak District Crime Thrillers

'Don't want to keep banging on but I sure hope you haven't given that job up for nothing, John.'

'What will be, will be, Vicky. My Dad always used to say that to me and Adam when we couldn't do something that he had asked us to do. 'Quitting? We don't much like quitters in these parts, Boy' I know he wasn't being nasty, just making us try harder.'

'Right guys, here are your starters.' Vicky and John stared in amazement at the portion sizes and the quality. Both plates and the mains were soon cleared.

After about fifteen minutes Doreen came back. 'You must try our new sweet menu, John, what about you my dear?'

'To be honest I will just have a brandy coffee please.'

'John?'

'I'll try the Mint Aero Bunny Trifle please, Doreen.'

It was almost 11.30pm when the bill was paid. Vicky thanked John for a nice evening and John saw his opportunity. 'Would you like a nightcap at mine, Vicky?'

Sad Man
Second in the series of the
John Gammon Peak District Crime Thrillers

'No, I'm fine, John, I am staying here tonight - I booked it early. Best at the moment, hey, while you sort yourself out.'

'Ok, Vicky, sleep well,' and John gave her a peck on the cheek. *Damn it,* he thought, *but maybe she is right, there is a lot still screwing with my life.*

Mrs Broadshaw had cleaned the cottage today and made the bed. John loved that part; he always said if he won the lottery the luxury of a fresh made bed would be one of his indulgences.

As usual, morning soon came and John was on the road to Bixton - not that he minded the drive, it was so beautiful - it was that he was just so desperate for some news on the killer and, of course, anything he could get on Lund.

John arrived at Bixton pretty much the same time as Dave Smarty. 'You are looking pleased with yourself.'

'I certainly am, Sir.'

'Come on then, share it.'

'Well, not had a lot of sleep, Sir, I staked out Lund's place until about 4am then at about 11.30pm last night, the Tink's Porsche pulled up at the gates and the gates were opened for him - he was at the house for about half an hour at most, then he, well think it was him, didn't get a clear view, he left so I followed the car. He drove for about forty minutes and then pulled over near Swallow Dyke, near Loke.'

'That's Staffordshire, isn't it?'

'Yes, Sir.'

'Then what?'

'Well from behind some trees, I saw a girl - I think it was Lola Thompson - she got in the Porsche and they drove off. I lost them at the other side of Loke, Sir.'

'There is enough there for me bring him in.'

'Yes, Sir.'

'Sergeant Hanney, is Scooper in yet?'

'Been here since 6.15am, Sir.' Gammon entered Scooper's office; she was busily looking through bank records of Mr Tink. 'There are some really unusual deposits and withdrawals, Sir.'

'Are these his business accounts or personal?'

'Personal, Sir, his business banking on the face of things looks ok but I'm not an accountant.' 'Understand, Sandra, just want to spot any anomalies. Then we can go from there.'

Sad Man
Second in the series of the
John Gammon Peak District Crime Thrillers

'Well, over the last year and a half, Tink has been withdrawing anywhere between £1000 to £2000 per week.'

'Ok, well he is a wealthy guy, why would he not?'

'That's it, Sir, he always takes it from the same branch at the same time every week.'

'Again, not seeing where you are going with this Sandra.'

'The branch he uses is directly opposite The Drovers Arms in Derby.'

'Now you are getting my attention.'

'There's more, Sir.'

'Go on.'

'He also has a standing order to a Miss Lola Thompson. I ran a background check on any Lola Thompsons known to us, and guess what that threw up? The bank account owner is called Miss Lola Thompson. I ran her name through the computer and I have a picture - she has a record for dealing and prostitution. I remembered you saying that when you went to Lund's house, everyone had alibis because of Lund's girlfriend!' Take a look at the picture, Sir, is that her?'

Sad Man
Second in the series of the
John Gammon Peak District Crime Thrillers

'Sandra, you are a diamond, that's her. Brilliant, Sandra, keep at it.'

As he came out of the office Sergeant Hanney said, 'Mr Tink is in the interview room with his solicitor and Sergeant Milton.' Gammon made his way to the interview room. On entering Milton informed the tape of his presence.

'Good morning, Mr Tink.'

'Mr Gammon, I have just lost my son in an horrific situation - both me and my wife are grieving and you want to question me? Wouldn't your time be better spent finding my son's killer?'

'Mr Tink, I can assure you that is what we are trying to do. When I first spoke with you, you could not remember the name of your son's girlfriend - you said 'I think her name is Lucy or Suzy or something', is that correct?'

'My son had plenty of friends.'

'Answer the question, Mr Tink.'

'Yes I may have said that, I can't remember.'

'Do you still own the Porsche that you told me that first night your son had borrowed?'

Sad Man
Second in the series of the
John Gammon Peak District Crime Thrillers

'Yes, why?'

'Can you tell me where you were last night?'

'At home with my dog.'

'Can anybody vouch for you?'

'Not unless my dog can talk.'

'Am I correct in saying you are a Professor in History and Science at the University of Derby?'

'You already know that, so why ask?'

'Well, Mr Tink, I find it a little strange that a professor has a show of such wealth. The Porsche, the big house, etc.'

'It is no business of yours what wealth I have.'

'Can you explain to me why you have a standing order from your bank in Derby to a Miss Lola Thompson?'

Tink's lawyer whispered in Tink's ear and he retorted, 'No comment.'

'Do you know who Lola Thompson is, Mr Tink?'

'No comment.'

Sad Man
Second in the series of the
John Gammon Peak District Crime Thrillers

'Well, Mr Tink, I am going to ask you something, then we will take a fifteen minute break so that you can decide if you wish to cooperate, which I seriously suggest you do. Last night, you were seen at Brian Lund's house - you were driving the Porsche,' and John tossed a couple of pictures that Inspector Smarty had taken. Tink was visibly shaken, and with that John suspended the tape.

Gammon and Milton left the room and headed for the coffee machine. 'He was shaken, Sir.'

'It is only a matter of time and he will crack. We will have this coffee then go back and find out what our Mr Tink is hiding.'

The interview reconvened. 'Well, Mr Tink, I assume you have had time to think.'

'Yes.'

'So why were you at Mr Lund's house?'

'Will my wife find out about any of this, Superintendent Gammon?'

Gammon knew he had Tink on the ropes. 'That will depend on what you tell me, Mr Tink.'

'About two years ago, my son Mark Anthony, brought this young girl home - she would have been nineteen; she was very pretty and she flirted with

Sad Man
Second in the series of the
John Gammon Peak District Crime Thrillers

me but only if we were ever left on our own. ,I am sorry to say I succumbed to her flirting and we started an affair.'

'Did your son know?'

'No, he didn't, Mr Gammon, and my wife must never know.'

'You need to open up and tell me everything, Mr Tink.'

'We started the affair and she was young and vibrant but she also had a cocaine habit. We would go to clubs and slowly she got me on it - that's how I got to know Brian Lund.'

Gammon was loving this. 'Go on, Mr Tink.'

'Well, about three months into the relationship, she said she had somebody who would like to meet me and this person had a big house with a swimming pool and he was having a big party. Anyway, I told my wife I was going to a University lecture in York so that I could spend the weekend with Suzy.

'We arrived at the party and there must have been at least a hundred people milling about; many of them skinny-dipping in Lund's swimming pool. I have to admit, I was quite high after a couple hours and Suzy took me upstairs. What I didn't know was that Lund was filming us.

'The next morning, most people had gone home and we were in his big kitchen when Lund came in. I can see him now; he was dressed in cream trousers and a pink shirt, his stomach hanging over his waistband. He had Lola Thompson on his arm. He asked me if we had a good time at his party. I thanked him for his hospitality and that's when he said I could do better than that. I replied 'excuse me' and then one of his henchmen hit me quite hard in the stomach. Suzy just laughed. She had set me up - I had been a silly old fool.

'Lund looked at me very menacingly; squeezing my cheeks together, he pointed at the 42" TV Screen on the kitchen wall. 'I am sure we all like a good film,' he said and they all started laughing. There on the big screen was me and Suzy - they had filmed us all night long, Mr Gammon. It was so embarrassing. By now, Suzy had left my side and was all over one of henchmen. I didn't know what was coming next; I got up to say I was leaving. Lund then looked at me and asked if the copies he had got would be better served by giving them to the University and my wife and golf club.

'I asked him what he wanted and he said as of now I would be his puppy is how he put it - I had to sell drugs on Campus and I also had to clean money through my bank account. He said I was to put it in then set up a direct debit for Lola Thompson - that way the money would be clean. If I was ever late or went to the police he would leak the videos. I didn't know what to do. I started doing what he asked of me. After four months he gave me some money that he said was bonus for my efforts - it was £10,000 but he said I mustn't put it into my normal account so I put it in to the building society. He started to regularly give smaller amounts which I kept putting away; my plan was to disappear one day when I had enough of his money.

'They planted Suzy on my son and I had to pretend I didn't know her after that night, and she got Mark into the drugs. The night she was murdered, I had been to see Tink at his house and he said Suzy was becoming a liability and either I would have to do something about her or he would. The next I knew, you were at my door telling me she was dead and you thought my son was involved.

'I panicked - this is my whole life here, Mr Gammon, I have already lost my son; that's why I went the other night to Lund's house - I went to confront him about Mark Anthony and to tell him I was finished with all this.'

'You were seen leaving and later a few miles away you picked a woman.'

Sad Man
Second in the series of the
John Gammon Peak District Crime Thrillers

'Lola Thompson was told to go with me to show me something. I had no choice. I picked her up after, down the road, and after a few miles she told me to stop the car. I did, and she played the audio to the video they had done of me and Suzy then she pulled a gun on me and said that they would first kill my wife then me if I uttered a single word about Brian Lund to anyone and that only Brian Lund will decide when enough was enough.'

'Will you testify in court?'

'I think I am ready, Mr Gammon, I have been stupid and this can't go on.'

'Ok, well, I suggest you go home tonight, get clothes and anything else you need packed for you and your wife and we will collect you in the morning. This guy is dangerous and we cannot take any chances, Mr Tink. Interview ended.' Tink and his solicitor left the room. Milton and Gammon felt really pleased, 'At last we have a solid witness.' 'We need to get Tink and his wife safely away, then we will arrest Lund.'

Gammon went immediately to Wills's office to tell her of the developments and to also get her to arrange the safe house.

Gammon left Bixton feeling at last he would avenge his brother and father. He drove straight past the

Sad Man
Second in the series of the
John Gammon Peak District Crime Thrillers

Spinning Jenny knowing he needed a good night's sleep before the arrest he had been wanting to make.

John tossed and turned for most of the night slightly in anticipation and also the thought that Lund had evaded him for so long now he was desperate to put him away; it was personal now.

John was back at the station by 7.30am; both Milton and Scooper were already there. 'Morning, you two, like me - couldn't sleep, hey.'

'The safe house people are going to ring me once they have picked the Tink's up.' Gammon got his obligatory cup of coffee or dishwater as he affectionately called it. He started wading through the mountain of mail. In the pile was a hand written letter so Gammon opened it first. It was from Claire Bryant.

Dear Mr Gammon,

Through my stupidity and my longing not to be lonely, I have not told you all about Jim Reynolds.

I met Jim at the Truck stop and he flirted with me, which I have to say I enjoyed at the time. Anyway, Jim found more and more loads down here and by

Sad Man
Second in the series of the
John Gammon Peak District Crime Thrillers

this time I had started to see him on a regular basis.
After a few months it seemed stupid him staying in
his lorry overnight so he moved in with me.
Everything was fine until one Saturday night; he said
he was going out with a couple of lads that were down
from the North East.

Anyway, Mr Gammon, he didn't come home until
almost five o clock on the Sunday morning. When I
asked him where he had been until this time he flew
into a rage, his eyes blurred and he seemed like he
was having a fit but he kept laughing. He was
strangling me and I thought I was going to die but my
dog Rex bit him and he let go, he kicked the dog so
hard we had to have him put down.

Then, for some reason, just like somebody had
flipped a switch, he was nice to me. I didn't say
anything in case he got violent again so I pretended
nothing happened. From that day I never questioned
where he had been or what he was doing. That way,
things were not too bad -he would slap me now and
again but you make excuses for people if you are
lonely. My daughter, Dana, said to me that she
thought he was weird - she had seen him in Bixton
and he was always trying to chat up her mates. She
said he had made comments to her when she had
been leaving the bathroom with her towel round her.

Sad Man
Second in the series of the
John Gammon Peak District Crime Thrillers

I am so sorry, Mr Gammon, if Jim turns out to be the man you are looking for but believe me I hid things about him because I was lonely and afraid of him.

I would prefer not to come to the station if possible; if he knew you were questioning me he would probably erupt again.

Claire Bryant

Gammon left his office to get Bradbury and Evans to bring Reynolds in. Just as they left the station, Sergeant Hanney called him over. 'Sir, we have a problem - Tink has been found hung in the woods near Micklock Moor.'

'Shit, Hanney, I can't believe my luck. Get forensics down there - I want some answers and quick.'

'Will do, Sir.'

Gammon went straight into Vicky's office to tell her the bad news. 'It's like every time we get a lead, this happens and as usual there isn't proof of anybody, especially Lund of any involvement.'

'John, I have had the Commissioner on - everyone is getting nervous that we don't have anyone in the frame for the rapes and murders on Micklock Moor. Where are we, John?'

Sad Man
Second in the series of the
John Gammon Peak District Crime Thrillers

'Look, Vicky, I think the Tink thing and the Micklock moor case are inexpiably linked.'

'John, I am not having a go, just want you to know they want to go National on this and possibly get Nottinghamshire and Yorkshire Police forces to pool resources.'

'That is stupid; we will have every nutter coming out of the woodwork.'

'I explained my sentiments are the same but they are giving us one week, then the Commissioner says he will have little choice but to bring them in.'

'Ok, Vicky, we will do our best but I still think it's stupid.' With that, Gammon left the room and assembled his squad - he had one last shot at solving the case. 'Right, I want discreet round the clock surveillance on Alison's house on Micklock Moor.'

'What are we looking for, Sir?'

'Well not bloody batman, Trimble! My gut feeling is; Miss Alison is not telling us everything, so please let's get out there now. Scooper, you sort the rota.'

Gammon decided to call it a night and headed up to his Mum's farm to ccc how she was; he hadn't been near since Uncle Graham had tried to make contact.

Sad Man
Second in the series of the
John Gammon Peak District Crime Thrillers

The beautiful surroundings always looked special at this time of night. John pulled into the yard. Roger Glazeback was just outside cleaning a bucket. 'Hi, Mr Gammon, you keeping well?'

'Pretty good thanks, Roger,' and John went inside. Emily was baking as was usual.

'Oh Mum, lemon drizzle cake, my favourite.'

'Sit down, son, I will cut you a piece, with a nice cup of tea.'

'Mum, you could enter competitions, this cake is fabulous.'

'I did win best Victoria sponge cake at Hittington-in-the-Dale Country show five years running.'

'Wow, bet that upset Betty Ingles?'

'You bet, John, that's why I stopped entering.' Typical Mum, always thinking of somebody else.

'So what do you know, Mum?'

'Well, Uncle Graham was a bit sad that you didn't come to see him.'

'I'm sorry, Mum, I have a lot on with the case and that.' Emily looked at him like only a mother can when they think their child is lying.

Sad Man
Second in the series of the
John Gammon Peak District Crime Thrillers

'Well the other thing I wanted was; we have to go to the solicitors for the reading of your Dad's will.'

'I didn't know he had one, Mum.'

'Oh yes, your Dad was precise about how things should be so we both made a will about fifteen years ago.'

'Ok, what time do we have to be there?'

'The solicitor said 3.00pm tomorrow.'

'Ok, Mum, should be ok. Do you know what is in Dad's will?'

'No, son, he never told me and I never asked. Just for the record, your Uncle Graham asked me if I would move up to his place and I told him I wouldn't - that this was my home until they carry me out in a wooden box.'

'How did he take that?'

'He said he wasn't surprised but the offer was always there if it was ever needed.'

'Ok, look Mum, I will pick you up tomorrow at 2.30pm - is it Flesner and Knapp, the solicitors, in Micklock?'

'Yes, that's correct, John.'

Sad Man
Second in the series of the
John Gammon Peak District Crime Thrillers

'Ok, Mum, see you then.'

'Lovely to see you, son.' John gave his Mum a kiss and set off for the Tow'd Man.

He arrived at the car park just as a balloon ride was taking off. Once inside, he quizzed Denis about the balloon; 'It's Cheryl's birthday and Bob got it for a surprise.'

'Has Bob gone with her?'

'Not likely, John, he said he doesn't like heights.' Just then Bob came in. 'What are you having, Bob?'

'I'll have a pint of Guinness please, John.'

'Guinness for Bob and a Pedigree for me please, Den and one for you.'

'I'll just have a pound with you, lad.' Denis never took liberties.

'So mate, when is next Pant's on Yer Head Bob performance?'

'I am at the Fox and Goose on Saturday - they have a band on and I am filling in when they take a break.'

'You will be famous one day Bob!'

Sad Man
Second in the series of the
John Gammon Peak District Crime Thrillers

'Would be nice, John, think of all that lovely money Cheryl could spend.'

'Get your thinking, Bob.' It was soon 10.30pm and John thought it best to call it a night. Jack and Shelley had just arrived with Carol Lestar and he could tell they would be on for a long night; they had been to a farm show and all looked well on their way already.

'Are you not stopping for one, my favourite Bobby?'

'Sorry, Carol, lot on tomorrow.'

'You are getting boring, John,' and she laughed.

'See you all soon,' and John made a quick exit.

On arriving at the cottage, he had a message on his phone from somebody. John clicked the voice message button. The voice on the other end appeared to be at some kind of party; he could hear people laughing and glasses chinking together. The voice just said 'hard luck again, Johnny Boy' then the phone went dead. He knew it was Lund. Gammon hated this guy but how can he ever prove any involvement if his witnesses keeping being killed with no trail back to the culprit?

The comfort of John's bed seemed to be over very quickly; his alarm was ringing and it was 7.15am.

Sad Man
Second in the series of the
John Gammon Peak District Crime Thrillers

John wandered to the shower. He shaved, cleaned his teeth and put his clothes on ready for work.

The journey to Bixton was always a beautiful drive, especially in the summertime. He stopped off at Beryl's Butties for his favourite Bacon sarnie. Beryl always put extra bacon on John's sandwich. He finished the sandwich and headed on to Bixton. John's mobile rang as he approached the station. 'Sir, we have had a development - we have found Jim Reynolds and he is here for questioning.'

'Great, thanks, Bradbury, I will be with you in a couple of minutes. Put Reynolds in interview room one, make sure he knows he can have a solicitor.'

John arrived at work and went straight up to see Vicky Wills. Gammon told Vicky they had arrested Reynolds and hopefully she may have some brighter news for the Commissioner. 'That would be good, John.'

'Right, I best get this sorted then.'

Gammon entered the interview room. Smarty and Scooper switched on the tape and went through the usual spiel.

Reynold's had refused a solicitor of his own or legal aid. He was dressed quite shabbily and he had a couple of days growth on; he looked like he had been sleeping rough.

'Right, Jim, we meet again.' Reynolds just looked at him - there was no feeling or sentiment in his eyes - he just stared at Gammon. 'So what happened to you then, Jim, are you sleeping rough?'

'I have been sleeping in my cab.'

'So you are no longer residing at Claire Bryant's place?'

'Correct, Gammon.'

'Did you two fall out?'

'Not that it is any of your business, but she constantly nags, so I left.'

'Did you give her a beating before you left, Jim?'

'No, is that what this is all about - has she said I hit her?'

'You like to keep your women in line with physical violence don't you, Jim?'

'What?'

'You like that power over them, don't you, Jim? Or should I call you Roy? Which is your real name?

Sad Man
Second in the series of the
John Gammon Peak District Crime Thrillers

Scooper had found that Roy Coors and Jim Reynolds were one and the same person. The police had been looking through the database for Jim Reynolds but he was actually called Roy Coors.

Coors had been convicted of rape and attempted murder by strangulation on a girl in Hartlepool in 1981; he got a nine-year sentence and was released after four years for good behaviour.

'So Jim, are you going to tell us why you attacked these girls and why you killed Suzy Warner? Were you disturbed?'

'I don't know what you are talking about. I made a mistake back in the 80s - that's why I changed my name, because you bastards will never let me live it down.'

'Don't you think it's a bit odd that since you have been in Derbyshire these poor girls have been raped and murdered with the same method you used on Sheila Walton?'

'I have no comment.'

'Well, I tell you what, Jim, I will be keeping you overnight before I decide if we are going to charge you, which I am pretty sure we will. Interview suspended,' and Gammon left the room.

Sad Man
Second in the series of the
John Gammon Peak District Crime Thrillers

He climbed the stairs and grabbed a coffee on the way to Vicky's office. 'Think we may have our man,' and Gammon went through the information Scooper had found on Roy Coors.

'John, this is great news.'

'He hasn't cracked yet, Vicky, but I'm sure he will.'

'Great, shall we go for lunch to celebrate?'

'Can't, Vicky, I have to go with Mum to the solicitors for the reading of my Dad's will. Perhaps tomorrow if we get a confession out of Reynolds, Coors or whoever he is.'

'Give Scooper a pat on the back from me, John, good detective work.'

'Will do, Vicky.'

John picked his Mum up at the farm and they drove down to the solicitors. Flesner and Knapp had been the family solicitors for many years. Mr Knapp was the guy John and Emily were seeing. When they arrived Mr Knapp's secretary informed Knapp they were here.

'Come in Emily, John, please take a seat.' The office was typical of a solicitors offioc; the seals were red leather chairs with a big red leather sofa and there were old pictures of the partners hanging

Sad Man
Second in the series of the
John Gammon Peak District Crime Thrillers

on the wall. May's desk was a big oak desk with a blue leather inlay and Mr May still wrote in ink - he had an ink pot on his desk and the ink pen next to it - *all very well organised,* John thought.

'First of all, I would like to say on behalf of myself and my partners how saddened we were at the untimely death of Philip. Philip re-wrote his will not long after Adam died; he was in sound mind and health which I vouched for.

'The contents of the will are as follows:

This is the last Will and Testament of Philip Adam Gammon:

    1. I revoke all previous wills made by me, Philip Adam Gammon

    2. Subject to the payment of my debts, funeral expenses and administration expenses, I give all my estate; both real and personal to my wife Emily Jane Gammon and appoint her sole executrix of this, my will.

    3. If my wife dies before me, or the gift to her shall fail for any other reason, then subject to payment of my debts, funeral expenses and administration expenses, I give all my estate both real and

Sad Man
Second in the series of the
John Gammon Peak District Crime Thrillers

personal to Roger Jack Glazeback, No3 The
Nook, Pritwich in Derbyshire.'

May carried on stating who the witnesses were and
the dates. John sat in shock; there was no mention
of him at all. May concluded the will reading and
Emily had to sign, which John witnessed.

Mr May then took an envelope out of his desk and
handed it to John. 'John, I have no idea what is in
the letter, I was just instructed by Philip to give you
this if he died before you. His only request was you
read it at some point when you were alone.

'Right, John, Emily, should you require any other
service from the partners, please let me know. I bid
you good day.' Emily and John never spoke until
they got in John's car in the car park.

'Are you all right, son?'

'Not sure, Mum, feel a bit stunned; not that Dad
didn't mention me in his will, but why? And this
letter - I want to do as he asked me - I will read it
tonight when I get back.'

'Look, son, the farm and everything is left to me and
you are sole beneficiary in my will. I don't know
why Dad would leave anything to Roger
Glazeback.'

Sad Man
Second in the series of the
John Gammon Peak District Crime Thrillers

Mum, he hardly knew him.'

'Well, that isn't going to happen, John, so please don't think bad of Dad - there may be some reason in your letter.'

John dropped his Mum off and went into his cottage. He poured himself a brandy knowing he wasn't going to like what he was about to read. He carefully opened the letter.

```
Dear John
If you are reading this then I have
left this earth. You will also be
wondering why my will was set up as it
was.

I will try and explain. Before you were
born, me and Mum were struggling. I
had over stretched myself with the farm
but knew one day it would work out.
Anyway, me and Mum had a row and your
Mum said she could no longer live like
we were doing so she left to spend some
time with her sister. As you know, I
can be pig headed but I was worried
about her so I asked your Uncle Graham
to pop by and see if she was ok. He
did and he assured me Emily would come
back - she just needed some space.

Your Mum eventually came back and in no
time she fell pregnant with you, John.
I was happy - we didn't have much money
and it was a struggle but I had what
```

Sad Man
Second in the series of the
John Gammon Peak District Crime Thrillers

all men want - a son to share the farm
with.

When you were seven or eight it became
noticeable that you didn't much look
like me. People would always be
remarking how you looked like my
brother Graham; at first I just thought
the Campbell gene was strong and we
laughed it off.

As you know, I always kept a diary and
at your eighteenth birthday party
everyone had a lot to drink and loads
of people kept saying about you and
Uncle Graham. I decided to check dates
and sure enough your Mum had come back
to me pregnant. I wrongly had a hair
from your uncle Graham and a hair from
you and I sent them off for DNA
analysis. My world fell apart when
they came back a perfect match. I
never said anything to your Mum or your
Uncle Graham but I hurt so much inside.
When you left home to join the police
force then eventually you moved to
London the pain subsided and I learned
to cope with the deceit.

I know none of this is your fault,
John, you are as much a victim as I am
but when I lost Adam I could not leave
my farm to a son who I know had no
interest and wasn't my real son

I hope you will eventually understand,
John, I tried very hard to be a good

Sad Man
Second in the series of the
John Gammon Peak District Crime Thrillers

```
father to you but my hurt will never go
away. Look after your Mum and if you
wish to share the letter that is your
decision.

Philip.
```

John slumped back in his chair, tears rolling down his cheeks; he felt sick. How could the man he loved and respected be so cruel at the end? He wished he had just thrown the letter away.

John decided to give Vicky a call. It seemed like ages before she answered. 'John?'

'Hi, Vicky.'

'Are you ok?'

'Not sure.'

'What is it - are you poorly?'

'No it was the will reading today, it was just a bit upsetting.'

'Where are you?'

'I am at my cottage.'

'Do you want me to come over?'

It would be nice to see a friendly face, Vicky.'

Sad Man
Second in the series of the
John Gammon Peak District Crime Thrillers

'Ok, I have only just left work so can be with you in twenty minutes.'

'Thanks, Vicky.'

'No problem,' and she ended the call.

John's Mum rang while he was waiting for Vicky. John just managed to hold it together. 'Are you ok, son?'

'Yes fine, Mum.'

'What did Dad say in the letter?'

'Oh he just asked me to look after you. That was all it was about.' He could hear the relief in Emily's voice.

'Well that was Dad - always worrying about me. So you are ok, son?'

'Yes, Mum, don't worry. You know Dad would not have meant anything by not including you in the will.'

'I know, Mum, its ok.'

'Ok then, son, try and get up to see me over the next few days.'

'I will, Mum, love you.'

Sad Man
Second in the series of the
John Gammon Peak District Crime Thrillers

'Love you too, Son.'

The conversation with his Mum finished just as Vicky was knocking on the cottage door. As usual, Vicky looked stunning; she had a black business suit on with a white shirt; her hair was long and wavy and she always reminded John of Julie Roberts in the film Pretty Woman.

John wiped his eyes. 'Whatever has happened, John? I have never seen you like this.'

'Oh the Will reading today - Dad never mentioned me, he left everything to Mum, which is fine, but he had said if Mum had died before him his estate was to be left to their farmhand, Roger Glazeback.'

'Oh, John, that must have hurt.'

'Well at the end, the solicitor gave me an envelope that Dad had left addressed to me only to be opened when I was on my own.' John handed the letter to Vicky; half way through she started to cry.

'Oh, John, I am so sorry for you.' Vicky put her arms round John and held him tight.

Before they both realised it, they were in John's bedroom; what had started as slowly being undressed turned into a frenzy; their insatiable appetite for each other was being fully played out. They made love more than once during that night then lay holding each other closely in silence both looking at the stars through the little cottage window.

John and Vicky fell to sleep and woke around 6.30am. John looked at Vicky with her long flowing auburn hair cascading down her naked back, her perfect, pure white skin soft to the touch. The words just came out, 'I love you, Vicky.'

Vicky reeled back, 'John this has to be a one-off, we are both building our careers from the last time - we have to just stay as friends. I have worked too hard, as you have, to throw it all away.'

'What if I took that job they offered me? Then I would be in a totally different environment and nobody could say anything.'

'John, you had the chance and the things that stopped you are still on the horizon so that would be a silly move.'

There wasn't much more to say and they pretty much left the cottage to climb into their respective cars to drive to Bixton.

'Sir, we have a guy here who has been waiting to see you. He said he will only speak with you.'

'Ok, what's his name?'

Sad Man
Second in the series of the
John Gammon Peak District Crime Thrillers

'Scott Gumm, he owns the stone cutting place behind Micklock Moor.'

Gammon wandered over to Mr Gumm. 'Mr Gumm, I'm Superintendent John Gammon, I believe you wish to speak with me. Would you like to come to my office?' Once in the office Gammon asked Gumm what this was all about.

'Well, Mr Gammon, I have a stone cutting place at the back of Micklock moor and what I have to tell you must not go any further. I have to periodically wash away all the dust from the cuttings - I have done it for many years, only it's not legal but nobody ever goes up there and, as I said, you must not breathe a word or they would shut me down.'

'What has this got to do with me, Mr Gumm?'

'Well this morning before all the blokes got here and while my cutting machines were off I started swilling down but the water would not go so I started to rod the stream. I still had no joy so I followed the stream. It came out about hundred yards away from that big old Alison house on the moor. Anyway I found what it was there was a load of old plastic bags that must have come from the quarry that had got stuck in the stream so I unblocked it but in the stream was a load of barbed wire also and I cut myself. The stream was unblocked and away it went. Round these parts

318

Sad Man
Second in the series of the
John Gammon Peak District Crime Thrillers

there has always been talk of a tunnel from the Alison House to close to what we call Alison drop where that lass was found. I just thought it was a load of rubbish but about ten yards passed the stream where it went underground I found a big wooden cover, and being nosey, I lifted it. It was very heavy but my curiosity needed fulfilling. Once I had lifted it I could see a ladder dropping about fifteen foot so I climbed down. The tunnel was dark and smelt damp so I could not see how far it went. To my horror, hung up at the bottom of the ladder was a beige coat like a rain mac with barbed wire sewn round it and there was a black ski mask with red lips. I bolted out of there, Mr Gammon.'

'Ok well thanks for that, Mr Gumm, your secret is safe with me and we will investigate.' Gammon could feel the elation running through his veins. He immediately informed Vicky and they decided to stake it out and wait to catch whoever came up with the clothes on out of the tunnel.

Gammon decided to let Reynolds go because if it was him then they would catch him in the act. The team of Gammon, Scooper, Milton, Trimble, Bradbury and Bannon camped out in the woods taking eight-hour turns at watching for the lid to lift and the guy to come out.

It was 10.00pm three nights later when the lid lifted on the tunnel; they radioed each other to keep

Sad Man
Second in the series of the
John Gammon Peak District Crime Thrillers

deadly quiet. A man approximately six feet four came out of the tunnel fully dressed in the clothes described. He looked all round him then started to walk. Gammon told everyone to stay back, 'I think he has a victim.' Sure enough, lay on the ground some three hundred yards across the moor was a young woman. Gammon gave the word; Milton was the first to get there and although he was badly cut by the barbed wire he managed to get the brute of a guy down and arrest him.

The poor girl had been walking her dog and was on holiday from Dorset and was not aware of the danger she was in. Di Trimble consoled her and everyone was taken back to Bixton Police Station. The young woman's parents, Mr and Mrs Grant, and their daughter, Joely Grant, were called and counselling was given.

Gammon had the guy out of the tunnel in the interview room. The tape started recording. 'Do you want a solicitor?'

'No thank you,' came the reply.

'Name?'

'Christopher Alison.' Gammon was surprised at the man's honesty; it wasn't until he listened further that he realised the guy appeared to be - as they say in

Sad Man
Second in the series of the
John Gammon Peak District Crime Thrillers

Derbyshire - a tomato short of a full salad - he wasn't overly clever as they say.

'Are you the man that has attacked these women on Micklock moor, Christopher?'

'Yes, Sir.'

'Did you kill Suzy Warner?'

'No, Sir, I never killed any of those ladies.'

The interview went on for a further three hours before Gammon had heard enough. 'Christopher Alison, I am charging you with the rape of Dana Bryant, Milam Peterson, Lara Bennett and Jane Wells; the abduction of Mary Denham; the murder of Sharon Bailey and the assault on Joely Grant. Do you wish to make a phone call?'

'Could I phone my Mum please?'

'Yes who is your Mum?'

'Meredith Alison, Sir.'

Gammon had already guessed that. 'Ok, let him have the call, then take him down, Scooper, and Bannon, bring Miss Alison in for questioning.'

'Yes, Sir.'

Sad Man
Second in the series of the
John Gammon Peak District Crime Thrillers

'Let me know when she arrives.' Gammon climbed the stairs to Vicky Wills's office. 'Good news, Vicky, we got him.'

'John, fantastic, are we sure?'

'We got him bang to rights - caught him in the act,' and he went through the full operation with Vicky.

'John, that is great, now the only minus is your concern with him - as you put it half a tomato short of a salad. Also, your concern that Suzy Warner may not have been raped and killed by Christopher Alison.'

'You know my feelings on that. Pretty sure Lund and his cronies are involved in that one and it was supposed to steer us of the scent.'

'Well let's see what Miss Alison says in the morning, John, and if we are sure I will inform the Commissioner and call a press conference.'

'Ok, Vicky. What are you doing tonight?'

'Not coming home with you - that was a one-off, John.'

'Ok, but you can't blame me for trying, Vicky.'

'Right, I'm calling it a day, did they release Reynolds?'

Sad Man
Second in the series of the
John Gammon Peak District Crime Thrillers

'Yes, while you were interviewing Christopher Alison.'

'Ok thanks, Vicky, goodnight.'

'Good night, John.'

John was feeling quite pleased with himself so he stopped off at the Spinning Jenny. 'Hi John, how are you, son?'

'Pretty good, Kev, what about you?'

'Still making a penny.'

'Wish I was a pound behind you.' Kev chuckled which made his red dickie bow jump up and down.

Carol Lestar was sat in the corner. 'Hi John, are you sitting with me after you have got me a drink?'

'Ok, Carol, what's it to be?'

'I'll have a pint of Guinness please.'

'So that's a pint of Guinness for Carol and I'll have a pint of Revolution.'

John sat down with Carol. 'Do you know what the ale is named after? It's a local brew.'

'No I don't, Carol, but I guess you are going to tell me.'

Sad Man
Second in the series of the
John Gammon Peak District Crime Thrillers

'The last revolution on English soil was started not far from here at Pentrich.'

'What, near Alfreton?'

'Yes.'

'You are kidding me.'

'No I went on a walk one Friday and the pub there has all these letters from the rebels to their families. It's a real good true story. There is a book out called the Last Revolution on English Soil.'

'I may get that, Carol, sounds interesting.'

John had a couple of hours with Carol then decided to call it a day. On the way home, he picked up the phone to Joni. As usual, Joni was her bubbly self. John felt a few pangs of guilt over Vicky the previous night. 'How are you, Joni?'

'I'm good thanks, John, just finished at the Wobbly - it was such a long night, hardly anybody in and I have an early start in the morning. We have a rare bird - a Little Ringed Plover - and it's nesting so we have to keep an eye on it, John.'

'Went right over my head, Joni, sorry. I will come out with you one day.'

'That would be really nice, John.'

Sad Man
Second in the series of the
John Gammon Peak District Crime Thrillers

'Anyway, what are you doing Saturday night?'

'I am off, John, and not planned anything yet.'

'Do you fancy going to the Fox and Goose? There's a group on and Bob is telling jokes in the interval.'

'Love to, John.'

'Ok, why don't you come to my place, say 7pm, and we can get a taxi and you can stop the night.'

'Ok, will see you Saturday.'

'Good luck with your Drover bird.'

'Bloody Plover, John, not Drover,' and they both laughed. The conversation ended and John arrived back at his cottage.

As John opened the door, he could see the letter he had left from his Dad on the kitchen table. John's mind started to race - should he destroy it or keep it? It was the only thing he had left of Philip and no matter what Philip had done, he knew it was because he was such a proud man and he thought he could relate to that.

Night turned in to day and very soon John was back at Rixton Police Station. 'Miss Alison is in interview room one with her solicitor, a Mrs Rosie Kirkton, Sir.'

'Ok which officers are in there?'

'Scooper and Milton.'

'Ok, thanks Sergeant.' John grabbed a coffee and entered the interview room. Scooper started the tape and spoke the procedure to be in the interview room.

Miss Alison was sat in a white blouse with a long black cardigan. She had her long straggly grey hair in a bun and she had a long black skirt on with what looked like gardening wellingtons on her feet.

Miss Kirkman was the opposite; she had red hair, was slim and tall in stature, and was wearing a brown business suit with a cream blouse and brown high heels.

'Good morning, everyone. As you are aware of the seriousness of your son's arrest, Miss Alison. Can I call you Meredith?'

Miss Alison had not lost any of her tenacity; she simply said, 'If you have too.'

'Ok, Meredith, last night we arrested a male, approximately fifty-eight years old; he was in the process of trying to rape a young woman on

Sad Man
Second in the series of the
John Gammon Peak District Crime Thrillers

Micklock moor about three hundred yards from your house. Meredith, he wore the same clothes and mask as described by all the previous victims.

'The question I have for you, Meredith, is; is Christopher Alison your son and does he live with you?'

Rosie Kirkman was quiet she was known to be possibly the top defence lawyer in Derbyshire. Meredith looked at Mrs Kirkman as if for guidance then Meredith broke down.

'Would you like a glass of water, Meredith?'

'No, I will be fine,' and she composed herself back to the bristling aggressive woman Gammon knew. 'Christopher contacted me three years ago; he had been living in America, well Kentucky, to be precise. His adopted parents moved there in the early sixties. It was out of the blue - his adopted mother had always told him about Derbyshire and me. I was so pleased. He asked if he could come and stay with me and of course I said yes. I am old now and the thought that my son who I had never seen after he was taken from me would want to stay with me was unbelievable.

'He finally arrived at the house some three years ago and has novor loft.'

Sad Man
Second in the series of the
John Gammon Peak District Crime Thrillers

'We searched the house, Meredith, we could not find any trace of him.'

'You wouldn't, Mr Gammon, there is a sliding bookcase that leads to a cellar and the tunnel. My father had it built many years ago.'

'So why was he hiding away?'

Meredith drew breath and Gammon could see she wasn't comfortable.

'Just answer the question, Meredith, please.'

'He was on the run; he told me that some girl had said he raped her but it was all lies but she was the sheriff's daughter and he said they would have thrown away the key - that he would not get a fair trial.'

'He never came up on police databases, Meredith.'

'He wouldn't - he called himself Michael Katts.'

'You do know that he has admitted to the crimes and has signed a written statement.'

'I thought he would, Mr Gammon, he is poorly - I am afraid he isn't the full shilling.'

'Meredith, I thank you for your cooperation but I am afraid we will have to charge you with harbouring a known criminal and obstructing the police in the course of their duties.

'That will do for now. Sergeant Milton, take her down.' Meredith was sobbing. Rosie Kirkman gave John the stare of *this won't stick in court* look.

Gammon reported to Vicky and she immediately rang the Commissioner and arranged a TV announcement for that night. 'John, I want you on the stage with me - I am sure we still have questions to answer on the Suzy Warner case and Mark Anthony Tink and his father.'

That night the interview was aired on National TV. John and Vicky held a good account to the public; they both realised that there were still three people dead; Suzy, Mark Anthony and Mr Tink which they had not solved. They assured the public that they would catch the person or persons responsible for the three unsolved murders.

John drove home feeling quite pleased with the results this far and knew he would have to work harder to get Brian Lund.

As John arrived at his cottage, Lund and two of his henchmon wcrc outside. 'What the hell do you want, Lund?'

Sad Man
Second in the series of the
John Gammon Peak District Crime Thrillers

'That's no way to speak to a friend, Johnny Boy. Me and the boys thought we would just pass a word of friendly advice onto you.

'There appears to be a lot of rapes and killings on your patch, Johnny Boy, and we have noticed you have a lot of pretty friends - especially that little barmaid you sniff round.'

'What are you saying, Lund?'

'Well, we thought it best to tell you to keep a close eye on your friends - we wouldn't want anything to happen to a friend of Johnny Boy now, would we, lads?'

They all started laughing. 'This is the last warning I will give you, Lund, get off my property and crawl back under the nearest stone you lump of shit.'

'Just being friendly, Johnny Boy, and looking out for you - good luck with your investigations.' With that, Lund sped away in his Mercedes.

John immediately phoned Vicky and explained what had happened. 'John, you know they will deny everything and there were three of them.'

'I tell you this, Vicky, I will get that bastard if it's the last thing I do - his reign of terror is coming to an end and fast.'

Sad Man
Second in the series of the
John Gammon Peak District Crime Thrillers

'I'm with you on that, John.'

John went into the cottage and made the decision to burn his Dad's letter; he never wanted his Mum to know.

He slumped back in his chair. What should have been a good day with the arrest of Christopher Alison now felt like a hollow victory. He wasn't sure if he wanted to carry on and maybe it was time to move on after all.

The End

Sad Man
Second in the series of the
John Gammon Peak District Crime Thrillers

Printed in Great Britain
by Amazon